Incredible Recipes
From a Prize-Winning
Recipe-Artist

A Taste You Can't Forget

Marylin Chong

Les Éditions Cuisiline Inc.
MONTREAL

© Copyright by Les Éditions Cuisiline Inc.
1993 first edition

All rights reserved. No part of this work may be reproduced or transmitted in any form or by any means, electronic or mechanical, including photocopying and recording, or by any information storage or retrieval system, without permission in writing from the publisher.

Canadian Cataloguing in Publication Data

Chong, Marylin

    A taste you can't forget

    Includes index.
    At head of title: Incredible recipes from a prize-winning recipe-artist.
    Issued also in French under title: Savoureuses escales.

    ISBN 2-9803414-1-X

    1. Cookery, International.   I. Title.

TX725.A1C4613 1993   641.59   C93-097130-2

Design and Layout by National Graphics Inc.

Printed in Canada

ISBN 2-9803414-1-X
Legal deposit - Bibliothèque nationale du Québec, 1993

To
My father, Louis-Albert,
Who, with Infinite Patience,
Instilled in me from my Earliest Years
a Respect and Appreciation
for the Great Variety of Food
our Native Island Has to Offer —
to him I Owe the Memory of the Profusion of Flavors
that Formed such an Integral Part of my Childhood;

To
my Daughter, Alexandrine,
my most Precious Treasure in this Wide World —

To
them both,
I Dedicate This Work
so that
from Generation to Generation
these Memories may Linger...

The Author wishes to express her appreciation to everyone who helped with this publication.

Special thanks to Vom Vadiveloo for his unfailing encouragement, to Robert Crerar for his many helpful ideas and for suggesting the title which now appears on the cover, to the people who took the pictures – Gui Schermer, Yassman Ameri, Gerald Schermer, Helmut Hausknost – to the small army of people who assisted with the purchases and preparation, and lastly, to her husband for his continuous support throughout this enterprise.

Canapés   Hors d'Oeuvres   Sandwichs

Crab and Fish Pâté (page 21)

Yellow Pea Rings — "Gâteau Pima"

Preparation time: 30 min.
Cooking time: 20 min.

1½ cups (310 g) yellow split peas
½ cup sliced green onion (scallion)
¼ tsp. baking powder
1 tsp. cayenne pepper
2 tbsp. milk
1¼ tsp. salt
⅓ cup (50 g) all-purpose flour
Vegetable oil
6 lettuce leaves

❶ Place the yellow peas in a **large** mixing bowl; rinse the peas with cold water. Drain and fill with cold water. Soak overnight in the refrigerator. Drain well.

❷ Crumble in a food processor until peas resemble fine uncooked couscous. The sides of the bowl of the food processor have to be scraped frequently during this process. Turn into the large mixing bowl.

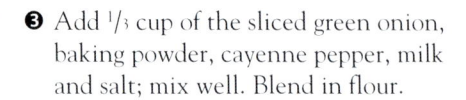

❸ Add ⅓ cup of the sliced green onion, baking powder, cayenne pepper, milk and salt; mix well. Blend in flour.

❹ Shape and press into 1-inch (2.5-cm) balls; then flatten lightly with the palms to obtain 1¾-inch (4-cm) circles. Form each ring by pressing the index finger through the center of the circle; deep-fry in hot oil until golden brown. Drain thoroughly on paper towels.

❺ Arrange the yellow pea rings on a serving platter lined with lettuce leaves and sprinkle with the remaining green onion.

❻ Serve warm or cold.

● Makes 26 rings.

Yellow Pea Rings — "Gâteau Pima"

Mont Choisy Rolled-up Bites

Preparation time: 20 min.
Cooking time: 25 min.

12 cooked crêpes (see page 54 "Morne Brabant Crêpes with Chicken and Chayote")
1 tbsp. vegetable oil
2 cloves garlic, finely chopped
1/2 lb. (225 g) bulk pork sausage
Dash of black pepper
4 cups finely chopped leeks
Pinch of curry powder
4 egg yolks, beaten

❶ Heat oil in a skillet over medium heat and sauté garlic.

❷ Add pork sausage and sprinkle with pepper. Cook, stirring constantly, for about 3 minutes. Toss in the chopped leeks and add curry; mix together until well blended. Cook for 3 to 5 more minutes, stirring frequently, until leeks are tender. Remove from heat.

❸ Brush each crêpe with beaten egg yolk. Spread a layer of leek mixture over crêpes and roll up each crêpe like a jelly roll.

❹ Brush the rolled crêpes with the remaining beaten egg yolk and place on a greased baking sheet. Bake in a preheated 350°F (175°C) oven for 8 to 10 minutes or until light golden brown.

❺ Cut each rolled crêpe crosswise into 4 equal pieces. Serve hot.

● Makes 48 appetizers.

Cheesy Zucchini Balls

Preparation time: 45 min.
Cooking time: 20 min.
(including the sauce)

3 cups grated zucchini
1 cup (100 g) grated mild cheddar cheese
1 1/3 cup (165 g) fine dry bread crumbs
1 clove garlic, finely chopped
1/4 cup (30 g) ground dried shrimp**
1 egg, beaten
1/4 tsp. salt
1/2 cup (70 g) all-purpose flour
Vegetable oil

** *Dried shrimp is available year-round in Chinese foodstores in packaged form. Using a food processor, grind finely.*

❶ Squeeze the grated zucchini to extract as much liquid as possible. You should obtain 2 cups of squeezed grated zucchini.

❷ Combine the zucchini, cheese, 1/3 cup of the bread crumbs, garlic, ground shrimp, beaten egg and salt. Mix together until well blended. Sprinkle with flour and blend until well absorbed.

❸ Take 2 tablespoons of mixture and shape into a ball; repeat this process with remaining zucchini mixture. Roll the balls in remaining bread crumbs to coat well. Heat oil in a frying pan and deep-fry the zucchini balls in the hot oil until golden brown. Drain well on absorbent paper.

❹ Serve the cheesy zucchini balls with spicy pineapple sauce (see recipe next page).

● Makes 20 appetizers.

The combined flavors of dried shrimp and cheese is surprisingly tasty.

Cheesy Zucchini Balls *(cont'd)*

SPICY PINEAPPLE SAUCE:

2 tsp. tapioca starch
1 cup (250 mL) pineapple juice
¼ tsp. garlic powder
¼ tsp. ground ginger
½ tsp. ketchup
Pinch of cayenne pepper
½ tsp. salt

❶ Combine tapioca starch with pineapple juice; pour into a non-stick saucepan and add remaining ingredients. Blend well and bring to a boil.

❷ Reduce the heat and cook, stirring until thickened. Cool and pour into a sauce-boat.

● Makes 20 servings.

Tropical Meatballs

Preparation time: 20 min.
Cooking time: 10 min.

¾ lb. (340 g) lean ground beef
2 tbsp. minced green onion (scallion)
2 cloves garlic, finely chopped
2 tbsp. minced onion
1 tsp. curry powder
¼ tsp. cayenne pepper
¼ cup (30 g) fine dry bread crumbs
½ cup (125 mL) whipping cream
¼ tsp. black pepper
¼ tsp. salt
Vegetable oil

❶ Combine all ingredients in a large bowl and mix well until thoroughly blended.

❷ Shape into 1-inch (2.5-cm) balls and deep-fry in hot oil at 350°F (175°C), tossing frequently until well browned.

❸ Drain on paper towels and arrange the meatballs on a lettuce-lined serving platter.

● Makes 28 appetizers.

Tropical Meatballs

Avocado Canapés

Preparation time: 40 min.
Cooking time: 10 min.

1 loaf sandwich bread, sliced
1 tbsp. butter
1 tbsp. minced green onion (scallion)**
$1/2$ cup (50 g) shrimp cocktail (canned), drained

❶ Using a wet cookie cutter, take the bread slices and cut out 2-inch (5-cm) sandwich circles. Place on a baking sheet and toast until browned. Remove from heat and let cool. Meanwhile, prepare the avocado cream.

** *Green onion is also widely known as shallot or scallion.*

Avocado Canapés (cont'd)

AVOCADO CREAM:

½ avocado, peeled
2 tsp. lemon juice
8 oz. (250 g) cream cheese, softened
½ tsp. garlic powder
¼ tsp. salt

❶ Mash enough avocado with a fork to obtain ⅓ cup (75 mL). Sprinkle with 1 teaspoon of lemon juice and mix thoroughly.

❷ Beat the cream cheese with garlic, 1 teaspoon of lemon juice and salt, using an electric mixer, until smooth. Fold in the mashed avocado.

❸ Chill for 30 minutes or until slightly firm.

❹ Meanwhile, melt butter in a skillet over high heat. Sauté green onion; add shrimp and cook for a few minutes, stirring. Set aside.

❺ Slightly beat the chilled avocado cream and spoon mixture into a pastry bag, fitted with a ¼-inch (6-mm) star nozzle. Pipe a rosette on each grilled sandwich round.

❻ Garnish with the sautéed shrimp.

● Makes 30 canapés.

Smoked Oyster Canapés

Preparation time: 35 min.
Heating time: 10 min.

12 slices sandwich bread
2 cups grated mild cheddar cheese
1 - 3.67 oz. (104 g) can smoked oysters

❶ Cut bread into circles, using a 2-inch (5-cm) wet fluted cutter. Cut an equal number of circles to match the number of oysters.

❷ Place bread-circles on a baking sheet and toast until light golden brown.

❸ Let cool. Divide 1 cup of grated cheese evenly between the toasted circles. Top with smoked oysters and divide the remaining cheese over all.

❹ Return to oven and broil at 350°F (175°C) for about 5 minutes or until the cheese becomes bubbly and the surface is golden brown.

❺ Serve hot.

● Makes 22 canapés.

These bubbly cheese canapés are not only easy to prepare but they are also delicious and your guests will surely enjoy them.

Brococrab Mousse

Preparation time: 30 min.
Cooking time: 15 min.
Refrigeration time: 4 to 5 hrs.

4 oz. (125 g) cream cheese, softened
2 cups (500 mL) milk
1 cup cooked broccoli flowerets, drained
4 oz. (113 g) crab meat
1 tbsp. minced green onion (scallion)
1 tsp. salt
2 envelopes (2 tbsp. or 14 g) unflavored gelatin
3 eggs, separated
Dash of white pepper
3 tbsp. white wine
1/4 cup (30 g) crushed graham crackers
6 pimento-stuffed green olives, sliced (to garnish)
Butter

❶ Place the cream cheese, milk, broccoli, crab meat, green onion and salt in an electric blender. Process at high speed until smooth.

❷ Turn into a saucepan and sprinkle with gelatin. Let soak for 5 minutes to soften, then dissolve over low heat, stirring.

❸ Beat the egg yolks and pour into saucepan. Stir in pepper and white wine. Bring to a boil; stir and cool.

❹ Chill mixture for 10 minutes.

❺ Grease an 8 1/2-inch (22-cm) springform pan with butter, then cover its bottom and sides with crushed graham crackers. Bring all excess crushed crackers around the outer edge of the pan, to thoroughly cover the joint. Refrigerate.

❻ Beat the egg whites until stiff, then fold into the cooled crab mixture. Pour into the prepared pan or into small ramekins, if desired (do not use crushed crackers in this case). Chill for about 4 hours or until set.

❼ Garnish with sliced olives and serve cold with croutons, bread sticks or toasted bread.

• Makes 6 to 8 servings.

Brococrab Mousse

Cucumber-Ham Appetizers

Preparation time: 15 min.

1 seedless cucumber
10 slices cooked ham
1 avocado, peeled, seeded and diced
Juice of 1 lemon
Cayenne pepper

So simple and easy to prepare and yet appealing. Requires no cooking at all.

❶ Make decorative stripes around cucumber, using a lemon stripper (canelle knife).

❷ Cut the cucumber thinly into ¼-inch (6-mm) slices.

❸ Cut out ham circles with a fluted 1-inch (2.5-cm) cutter.

❹ Drizzle the diced avocado with lemon juice to prevent discoloration. Drain.

❺ Arrange two ham circles on each slice of cucumber and top with diced avocado. Sprinkle lightly with cayenne pepper, if desired.

● Makes 30 appetizers.

Flic-en-Flac Pouches

Preparation time: 25 min.
Cooking time: 55 min.

17

Flic-en-Flac Pouches *(cont'd)*

BATTER:

1 egg
Pinch of salt
1 cup (140 g) flour
1 1/3 cups (325 mL) milk
1/4 cup (60 mL) melted butter

❶ In a mixing bowl, beat egg and salt with an electric mixer. Gradually and alternately add flour and milk, beating at a slow speed until smooth.

❷ Fold in melted butter.

❸ Chill at least one hour before using.

❹ Place a small non-stick skillet over medium heat and brush with butter. Pour in 1 3/4 tablespoons of batter. Lift and tilt the skillet in a circular motion in order to spread batter over the bottom of the skillet. Cook until light golden brown; carefully turn the crêpe with a plastic spatula and cook the other side. There is no need to grease the pan for cooking remaining batter.

❺ Line mini-muffin pans with the crêpes. Set aside.

REMARK: Crêpes can be stored in the refrigerator for about 3 days, when properly wrapped in foil or plastic, and up to 2 months in the freezer. Use wax paper to separate them and freezer bags or freezer containers for storage in the freezer.

Flic-en-Flac Pouches (cont'd)

FILLING:

2 tbsp. butter
1 clove garlic, minced
1 tbsp. finely chopped onion
1 tbsp. minced green onion (scallion)
1 - 4.2 oz. (120 g) can crab meat, drained (reserve ¼ cup [60 mL] broth)
Pinch white pepper
2 tbsp. all-purpose flour
¾ cup (170 mL) milk
1 egg
2 egg yolks
Pinch curry powder
Dash Tabasco
¼ tsp. salt
6 cherry tomatoes, cut into small pieces

❶ Melt butter over medium heat in a skillet. Sauté garlic, onion, and green onion. Add the drained crab meat; sprinkle with pepper and cook for a few minutes, stirring.

❷ Sprinkle flour over mixture and blend well. Add broth and milk; cook for a few minutes over low heat, stirring until thickened. Remove from heat.

❸ Beat the egg and egg yolks lightly, then fold into the crab mixture. Add curry powder, Tabasco and salt. Mix thoroughly.

❹ Pour into the mini-muffin pans lined with crêpes to ⅔ depth and sprinkle pieces of tomatoes atop. Bake in a preheated 350°F (175°C) oven for 12 to 15 minutes or until a wooden pick inserted in center comes out clean.

● Makes 24 pouches.

Tarragon Meat Pouches

Preparation time: 70 min.
Cooking time: 30 min.

DOUGH:

1 cup (250 mL) milk
¼ tsp. sugar
2 packages (8 g each) active dry yeast
4 cups (550 g) all-purpose flour
Pinch salt
½ cup (120 g) butter
2 eggs

❶ Warm milk in a small saucepan and sprinkle with sugar and yeast. Let stand for about 10 minutes or until frothy. Stir gently.

❷ Melt butter and let cool slightly.

❸ Meanwhile, sift flour and salt in a large mixing bowl and shape into a ring. Pour the milk and yeast mixture in the center of the ring.

Tarragon Meat Pouches (cont'd)

❹ Lightly beat the eggs together with melted butter and pour mixture in the center of the flour ring. Mix with a fork, then knead for 5 to 10 minutes or until dough is smooth.

❺ Cover with cloth and let rise in a warm place for about one hour.

FILLING:

³/₄ lb. (340 g) lean ground beef
Dash of black pepper
1 small onion, finely chopped
2 tbsp. tarragon
¹/₄ cup (30 g) fine dry bread crumbs
¹/₂ cup (125 mL) whipping cream
¹/₂ tsp. salt
2 eggs, beaten

❶ Place the beef in a large mixing bowl and season with pepper. Add remaining ingredients except the beaten eggs and mix thoroughly.

❷ Roll out dough into an 18-inch square (46-cm) on a floured surface. Divide into 6 long strips of 3 x 18 inch (8 x 46 cm) and cut equally into 3-inch (7.5-cm) squares.

❸ Divide the filling evenly between the dough squares. To form each pouch, take all the edges of a square with fingers and, with a circular motion, press firmly to seal.

❹ Brush the pouches with beaten eggs and place on a greased baking sheet. Bake in a preheated 400°F (200°C) oven until golden brown (25 to 30 minutes).

● Makes 36 pouches.

Crab and Fish Pâté

Preparation time: 15 min.
Cooking time: 60 min.

½ lb. (225 g) crab meat
½ lb. (225 g) bluefish, cut into pieces
½ cup (125 mL) milk
2 cloves garlic, coarsely chopped
1 small onion, coarsely chopped
1 tbsp. green onion (scallion), chopped
1¾ cups (420 mL) whipping cream
1 tsp. salt
¼ tsp. white pepper
3 cups (360 g) fine dry bread crumbs
¼ cup (60 mL) tomato paste
3 eggs
2 egg yolks
3 hard-boiled eggs, cut into ¼-inch (6-mm) slices (to garnish)
Capers, drained (to garnish)
1 bunch of watercress (to garnish)

❶ Place the crab, bluefish, milk, garlic, onion and green onion, ½ cup (125 mL) cream, salt and pepper in a food processor. Process at high speed until smooth. Turn into a large mixing bowl.

❷ Add bread crumbs, tomato paste and the remaining cream; mix together until well blended.

❸ Lightly beat all the eggs together and fold into the mixture.

❹ Grease a loaf pan with butter and spoon the mixture into the pan. Smooth the surface evenly. Place the loaf pan in a larger baking pan and fill the larger pan with hot water to a depth of 1 inch (2.5 cm).

❺ Bake in a preheated 350°F (175°C) oven for about 1 hour or until a wooden pick inserted in the center comes out clean. Cover loosely with aluminum foil after baking 45 minutes.

❻ Top with overlapping egg slices and garnish with capers and watercress.

❼ Serve warm or cold.

● Makes 8 servings.

Oriental Beef and Pepper Sandwich

Preparation time: 15 min.
Cooking time: 13 min.

½ lb. (225 g) sirloin, shredded
1 tbsp. light soy sauce
¼ tsp. black pepper
2 tbsp. tapioca starch
¼ cup (60 mL) vegetable oil
1 clove garlic, chopped
1½ tsp. finely chopped ginger
1 green pepper cut into thin strips
1 red pepper cut into thin strips
1 cup (250 mL) water
Salt
1 thin loaf French bread - "baguette"

❶ Drizzle the meat with soy sauce; sprinkle with pepper and 1 tablespoon of tapioca starch; mix thoroughly to coat well.

❷ Heat 3 tablespoons of oil over medium heat in a skillet and sauté garlic and ginger for 1 minute. Add the shredded beef and cook over medium-high heat, stirring constantly for 3 minutes until browned. Remove from skillet and keep warm.

❸ In the same skillet, heat 1 tablespoon of oil and sauté green and red peppers over high heat, stirring until crisp-tender. Lower the heat to medium. Combine the remaining tapioca starch with water and pour into the skillet. Cook, stirring until sauce thickens. Add salt to taste.

❹ To make the bread more crispy, heat in a preheated 350°F (175°C) oven for 5 minutes. Allow to cool; split, then stuff with beef and peppers together with the sauce.

❺ Cut the bread diagonally into 1½-inch (3.5-cm) slices.

● Makes 20 appetizer-sandwiches.

Chicken-Bacon Sandwich

Preparation time: 15 min.
Cooking time: 10 min.

1 chicken breast, skinned and boned
Pinch of salt
Pinch of white pepper
4 slices bacon
1 tbsp. butter
1 clove garlic, finely chopped
½ cup (125 g) cream cheese, softened
3 tomatoes, sliced
4 lettuce leaves, shredded
4 small round "Kaiser" buns, plain or whole wheat

❶ Season chicken with salt and pepper. Pound lightly with a meat mallet and then cut into bite-sized pieces.

❷ Chop the lean part of the bacon.

❸ Melt butter over medium heat in a non-stick skillet and sauté garlic for one minute. Add chicken and bacon and cook for 4 to 5 minutes, stirring until the meat is done.

❹ Add the cream cheese and melt thoroughly over low heat, blending well. Remove from skillet and keep warm.

❺ Heat the mini-buns in a preheated 350°F (175°C) oven until crispy (5 minutes). Let cool, then split horizontally. Spoon half cup of creamy chicken-bacon mixture over each bottom half of bread, then top with a few slices of tomato and shredded lettuce. Cover with the other half of the bread.

• Makes 4 sandwiches.

REMARK: When cut in quarters and filled with this savory and creamy chicken-bacon mixture, these appealing canapés are ideal for any occasion.

Chicken-Celery Sandwich

Preparation time: 15 min.
Cooking time: 15 min.

1 chicken breast, skinned and boned
2 tbsp. butter
1 tbsp. onion, coarsely chopped
1 clove garlic, finely chopped
1½ cups or 2 stalks celery, cut diagonally into thin slices
½ tbsp. tapioca starch
½ cup (125 mL) milk
⅓ cup (75 mL) sour cream (optional)
¼ tsp. Worcestershire sauce
Dash Tabasco
1 tsp. dried parsley flakes
White pepper
Salt
4 small round "Kaiser" buns, plain or whole wheat

❶ Pound the chicken breast with a meat mallet. Season lightly with salt and pepper, then shred or cut into small pieces.

❷ Melt butter over medium heat in a non-stick skillet and sauté onion and garlic for one minute. Add the chicken and cook for 4 to 5 minutes, stirring until done. Remove from skillet and keep warm.

❸ Sauté the celery in the skillet drippings, stirring frequently, until tender. Reduce heat and remove from skillet.

❹ Combine tapioca starch with milk, then pour into the skillet. Add the sour cream, Worcestershire sauce, Tabasco and parsley flakes. Blend thoroughly and cook over low heat, stirring until thickened. Return the chicken and celery to the skillet and mix together.

❺ Add salt to taste.

❻ Heat the mini-buns in a preheated 350°F (175°C) oven for 5 minutes. Allow to cool; split horizontally and then divide the creamy chicken-celery mixture equally between the bottom halves of the mini-buns. Cover with the other half of the bread.

● Makes 4 sandwiches.

Salmon and Egg Sandwich

Preparation time: 8 min.
Cooking time: 10 min.

4 eggs
1 cup (100 g) grated mild cheddar cheese
1 tbsp. dried parsley flakes
2 tbsp. vegetable oil
1 small onion, chopped
1 - 7.6 oz. (213 g) can pink salmon, drained
3 tomatoes, sliced and halved
1 bunch watercress
1 thin loaf French bread - "baguette"
White pepper

❶ Beat the eggs with a dash of pepper; add cheese and parsley and mix together.

❷ Heat oil over medium heat in a skillet and sauté onion for one minute. Add the salmon; sprinkle lightly with pepper and cook, stirring constantly, for 2 minutes.

❸ Pour the egg mixture into the skillet and cook for two minutes, blending thoroughly, until mixture becomes crumbly. Remove from heat and keep warm.

❹ To make the bread more crispy, heat in a preheated 350°F (175°C) oven for 5 minutes. Allow to cool. Split the bread horizontally, then stuff it with the salmon and egg combination. Top with sliced tomatoes and watercress.

❺ Cut bread diagonally into 1-inch (2.5-cm) slices and serve immediately.

● Makes 18 appetizer-sandwiches.

REMARK: *These bites make excellent canapés. They are ideal for brunches, buffets or picnics.*

Tuna and Tomato Sandwich

Preparation time: 15 min.

1 - 6.5 oz. (184 g) can flaked tuna, drained
2 tbsp. olive oil
1 tbsp. finely chopped onion
Dash of black pepper
Juice of half a lemon
1 tbsp. vinegar
2 tsp. dried parsley flakes
Mayonnaise
Pinch of salt
2 or 3 tomatoes, sliced
2 cups alfalfa sprouts
8 slices rye bread

❶ In a small mixing bowl, combine tuna, olive oil, onion, pepper, lemon juice, vinegar, parsley, 2 tablespoons of mayonnaise and salt. Mix well.

❷ Toast the slices of bread until golden brown (optional) and then spread mayonnaise on each of them.

❸ Divide the tuna mixture equally between four of the bread slices, then top with 1 or 2 slices of tomato. Sprinkle thickly with alfalfa sprouts and cover with the remaining slices of bread.

❹ Cut the sandwiches in half and serve immediately.

● Makes 4 sandwiches.

Sausages with Honeydew and Cantaloup

Preparation time: 45 min.

1 cantaloup
1 honeydew melon
Juice of 1 lemon
3 - 4 oz. (113 g) cans Vienna sausages, drained

❶ Cut the cantaloup and melon in half, then remove all the seeds. Scoop out balls with a Parisian cutter. Drizzle with lemon juice; drain well and set aside.

❷ Cut the sausages in three, crosswise.

❸ Count out equal quantities of cantaloup and honeydew fruit balls to equal the number of sausages. Slice all the balls in half. Place a sausage between a halved fruit ball on a wooden pick. Repeat until all sausages are used.

❹ Chill. Remove from refrigerator 15 minutes before serving.

● Makes 63 appetizers.

These hearty and easily prepared appetizers require no cooking at all.

Beef Tartlets

Preparation time: 25 min.
Cooking time: 35 min.

SHELL:

14 oz. (397 g) frozen puff pastry, thawed

❶ Roll out pastry dough to 1/8-inch (3-mm) thickness on a slightly floured surface and line 22 tartlet pans. Prick shells all over with a fork.

❷ Set aside.

FILLING:

1 tbsp. butter
1 clove garlic, minced
2 tbsp. onion, finely chopped
2 cups finely chopped leeks
1/2 lb. (225 g) lean ground beef
1 tbsp. flour
1/2 cup (125 mL) milk
3 eggs, lightly beaten
1/2 tsp. salt
1/4 tsp. black pepper
1 cup (100 g) grated mild cheddar cheese
Parsley sprigs (to garnish)

❶ Melt butter in a skillet over medium heat and sauté garlic, onion and leeks for 2 minutes.

❷ Add beef and cook, stirring constantly, until browned. Stir in flour and milk until well blended. Remove from heat and fold in the beaten eggs. Season with salt and pepper.

❸ Spoon mixture into the tartlet shells and sprinkle tops with cheese. Bake in a preheated 400°F (200°C) oven for 15 minutes.

❹ Garnish with parsley sprigs and serve hot.

● Makes 22 tartlets.

Salads

Avocado Salad with Peanut Butter Vinaigrette (page 30)

Avocado Salad with Peanut Butter Vinaigrette

Preparation time: 10 min.

SALAD:

2 firm ripe avocados, peeled, seeded and diced
3 cups watercress
2 tomatoes, sliced
½ seedless cucumber, sliced and halved
4 tbsp. minced chives
Juice of 1 lemon

❶ Drizzle the diced avocado with lemon juice; drain.

❷ Arrange the watercress at the bottom of a salad bowl.

❸ Add the diced avocado, tomatoes and cucumber. Mix gently.

❹ Spoon vinaigrette over all and sprinkle with minced chives.

● Makes 4 servings.

PEANUT BUTTER VINAIGRETTE:

3 tbsp. olive oil
Juice of one lemon
2 tbsp. wine vinegar
1 tbsp. peanut butter (creamy)
Pinch of thyme
Pinch of dried parsley flakes
1 clove garlic
1 tsp. black pepper
½ tsp. salt

❶ Put all the ingredients in an electric blender and process until smooth.

● Makes ½ cup (125 mL) of vinaigrette.

Okra Salad

Preparation time: 10 min.
Cooking time: 8 min.

4 cups okra
½ seedless cucumber
2 tomatoes
1 cup watercress
1 cup bean sprouts
1 recipe "Peanut Butter Vinaigrette", page 30

❶ Remove tops from okra and steam until tender. Cut them into ½-inch (12-mm) pieces.

❷ Thinly slice the cucumber and the tomatoes.

❸ Arrange all the vegetables in a salad bowl and mix gently.

❹ Spoon the peanut butter vinaigrette over all and toss until vegetables are well coated.

• Makes 4 servings.

Tropical Salad

Preparation time: 10 min.

1 half-ripe mango, peeled and diced
1 seedless cucumber, sliced and halved
1 medium carrot, sliced
1 bunch watercress, separated
2 tomatoes cut into wedges
1 recipe "Hot Pineapple Vinaigrette", page 33

❶ Toss all the ingredients in a salad bowl and mix gently.

❷ Pour hot pineapple vinaigrette over all and toss to coat well.

• Makes 4 servings.

Carambola Star Salad

Preparation time: 15 min.

SALAD:

3 ripe carambolas, thinly sliced
1 seedless cucumber, sliced and halved
1 - 15 oz. (426 mL) can baby corn, sliced in two – lengthwise
2 tomatoes, sliced
Lettuce torn into pieces
1 cup alfalfa sprouts

VINAIGRETTE:

1/3 cup (75 mL) olive oil
3 tbsp. wine vinegar
1 tbsp. lime juice
1 tbsp. finely chopped onion
1/2 tsp. salt
Dash of black pepper

❶ Arrange all ingredients except the alfalfa sprouts in a salad bowl. Mix gently. Sprinkle with alfalfa sprouts.

❷ Pour vinaigrette over all.

● Makes 4 servings.

❶ Mix all ingredients together until well blended.

● Makes 2/3 cup (150 mL) of vinaigrette.

Water Chestnut Salad

Preparation time: 15 min.

1 small fresh pineapple, skinned and sliced or 1 - 10 oz. (284 mL) can pineapple rings, drained
2 - 8 oz. (227 mL) cans water chestnut, sliced and drained
2 tomatoes, quartered and sliced
Lettuce, torn into large pieces
A few spinach leaves

❶ Line the bottom of a salad bowl with spinach leaves.

❷ Cut the pineapple rings into pieces.

❸ Toss in the pieces of pineapple, water chestnut, tomatoes and lettuce.

❹ Pour hot pineapple vinaigrette over all and toss to mix well.

● Makes 4 servings.

HOT PINEAPPLE VINAIGRETTE:

$1/2$ cup (125 mL) pineapple juice
2 tbsp. olive oil
2 cloves garlic
1 tbsp. lemon juice
1 tbsp. lime juice
1 tsp. salt
$1/4$ tsp. white pepper
$1/2$ tsp. Tabasco
1 tsp. honey

❶ Place all ingredients in an electric blender and process until smooth.

● Makes 1 cup (250 mL) of vinaigrette.

Artichoke-Corn Salad

Preparation time: 10 min.

SALAD:

6 Boston lettuce leaves
1 - 15 oz. (426 mL) can artichoke hearts, drained
1 - 15 oz. (426 mL) can baby corn, drained
3 sliced tomatoes
5 pimento-stuffed green olives, chopped

❶ Line a salad bowl with lettuce and arrange all ingredients in the bowl. Sprinkle with chopped olives and pour chestnut vinaigrette over all.

❷ Toss lightly to mix and serve.

● Makes 4 servings.

CHESTNUT VINAIGRETTE:

$2/3$ cup (150 mL) olive oil
2 tbsp. chestnut purée
1 tbsp. chopped onion
Pinch of thyme
$1/4$ tsp. black pepper
1 tbsp. lemon juice
$1/2$ teaspoon salt

❶ Place all ingredients in a blender and process until smooth.

● Makes 1 cup (250 mL) of vinaigrette.

Beet and Potato Egg Salad

Preparation time: 12 min.
Cooking time: 45 min.

SALAD:

3 small or 2 medium-sized beets
2 medium potatoes
3 hard-boiled eggs, sliced
1 white onion, sliced and separated into rings

❶ Cut ends off beets.

❷ Cook separately the unpeeled beets (45 minutes), and the unpeeled potatoes (30 minutes) or until tender in lightly salted boiling water. Drain and cool.

❸ Peel and cut into pieces. Place in a salad bowl and arrange the egg slices and onion rings on top. Spoon vinaigrette over all and mix to coat well.

● Makes 4 servings.

REMARK: This salad can be prepared in advance. Refrigerate the potatoes and the beets in separate bowls until ready to serve; add eggs and onion slices at the last moment.

VINAIGRETTE:

2 tbsp. olive oil
2 tbsp. vinegar
Dash of black pepper
¾ tsp. salt

❶ Combine all ingredients and stir until well blended.

● Makes ¼ cup (60 mL) of vinaigrette.

Hearts-of-Palm Island Salad

Preparation time: 15 min.

SALAD:

1 - 14 oz. (398 mL) can hearts of palm, drained
Skinless sections of half a grapefruit
1 green pepper, seeded and shredded
1 red pepper, seeded and shredded
6 Boston lettuce leaves

❶ Line a salad bowl with lettuce.

❷ Thinly slice the hearts of palm and place over the lettuce leaves. Add the grapefruit sections as well as the shredded green and red peppers.

❸ Pour vinaigrette over all and toss to mix well.

● Serves 4.

VINAIGRETTE:

½ cup (125 mL) olive oil
Juice of one lemon
2 tbsp. wine vinegar
1 clove garlic, minced
2 tbsp. chopped onion
2 tsp. salt
2 tsp. sugar
Pinch of black pepper
Pinch of dried crushed chili pepper

❶ Combine all ingredients in an electric blender and whirl until smooth.

● Makes ¾ cup (170 mL) of vinaigrette.

Soups

Cream of Corn and Leek Soup (page 38)

Cream of Corn and Leek Soup

Preparation time: 15 min.
Cooking time: 40 min.

2 slices bacon
2 tbsp. butter
1 clove garlic, minced
1 cup chopped white leeks
1 cup (250 mL) milk
⅓ cup (75 mL) canned cream-style corn
3 cups (750 mL) chicken broth
¼ cup (60 mL) white wine
1 small potato, peeled and diced
Pinch of paprika
Dash Worcestershire sauce
¼ cup (60 mL) whipping cream
Salt
Parsley sprigs (to garnish)

❶ Trim fat from bacon and chop the lean portion coarsely.

❷ Melt butter in a medium saucepan and sauté garlic and bacon. Add chopped leeks and cook over medium heat, stirring until leeks become slightly transparent.

❸ Stir in milk, corn, chicken broth and white wine. Add the diced potatoes. Bring to a boil and cook, stirring frequently, for 5 minutes.

❹ Cool and process to a smooth purée in blender. Return to saucepan and bring to a boil. Season with paprika and Worcestershire sauce.

❺ Reduce the heat and simmer for 20 minutes. Add salt to taste.

❻ Pour a tablespoon of whipping cream in the center of each serving and garnish with a sprig of parsley.

● Makes 4 servings.

See photograph on page 37.

Spinach Soup with Fish

Preparation time: 12 min.
Cooking time: 25 min.

1 1/2 cups chopped spinach
2 cups (500 mL) chicken broth
1 tbsp. oil
2 cloves garlic, finely minced
1 tbsp. chopped onion
1 cup diced fish fillet (bluefish)
1/3 cup (75 mL) white wine
1 tomato, peeled and chopped
1 egg
Salt

❶ Purée spinach and chicken broth in a blender until smooth.

❷ In a large saucepan, heat 1 tablespoon of oil over medium heat and sauté garlic and onion. Throw in the diced fish and cook, stirring, for 3 to 5 minutes.

❸ Pour in the wine and mix well.

❹ Blend in the chopped tomato and spinach purée. Bring to a boil. Break in the egg and stir vigorously to crumble. Lower the heat and simmer for 10 minutes.

❺ Add salt to taste.

● Makes 4 servings.

Chayote Soup with Clams

Preparation time: 8 min.
Cooking time: 25 min.

1/2 chayote, peeled and seeded
1 tbsp. vegetable oil
2 cloves garlic, finely chopped
1 tbsp. onion, finely chopped
1 - 5 oz. (142 g) can baby clams, undrained
1/4 cup (60 mL) dry white wine
2 tbsp. cornstarch
1 cup (250 mL) milk
2 cups (500 mL) chicken broth
1/3 cup (75 mL) tomato sauce
1/3 cup finely chopped celery
Salt
4 tablespoons minced parsley

Chayote Soup with Clams *(cont'd)*

❷ Heat oil in a large heavy saucepan and sauté garlic and onion over medium heat.

❸ Add the chayote and cook, stirring, for 3 minutes. Pour in the clams together with the broth. Stir and cook for 3 to 5 minutes.

❹ Add wine and blend well.

❺ Combine cornstarch with milk and pour into the saucepan. Add chicken broth, tomato sauce and celery. Bring to a boil. Lower the heat and simmer for 15 to 20 minutes.

❻ Add salt to taste.

❼ Sprinkle with minced parsley.

❶ Slice the chayote and chop finely.

● Makes 4 servings.

Cauliflower Soup with Crab

Preparation time: 5 min.
Cooking time: 40 min.

1 cup cauliflower flowerets
2½ cups (625 mL) chicken broth
1 tomato, peeled and chopped
1 clove garlic, finely chopped
1 tbsp. butter
1 tsp. minced green onion (scallion)
4 oz. (115 g) crab meat
¼ cup (60 mL) white wine
1 cup (250 mL) milk
Salt
White pepper
4 tablespoons finely chopped parsley

Cauliflower Soup with Crab (cont'd)

❶ Place the cauliflower, chicken broth and tomato in a saucepan. Bring to a boil; reduce the heat and cook for 10 minutes or until tender. Cool.

❷ Meanwhile, in a skillet, sauté garlic in butter over medium heat. Stir in the green onion. Add the crab meat and mix until well scattered. Cook for a few minutes, stirring constantly, then pour in the white wine and milk. Blend well. Let cool slightly.

❸ Pour into a blender, then add the cauliflower-tomato mixture. Process at high speed until smooth and return to saucepan. Bring to a boil. Lower the heat and simmer for 15 minutes.

❹ Add salt and pepper to taste.

❺ Sprinkle with chopped parsley and serve.

• Makes 4 servings.

Crab Soup with Vegetables

Preparation time: 13 min.
Cooking time: 25 min.

2 slices bacon
1 tbsp. vegetable oil
1 tbsp. finely chopped onion
1 clove garlic, finely chopped
¼ cup (60 mL) dry white wine
2 cups (500 mL) chicken broth
½ cup chopped celery
1 small potato, peeled and diced
2 - 4.2 oz. (120 g) cans crab meat, undrained
¼ cup (60 mL) tomato sauce
2 tbsp. whipping cream
1 cup (250 mL) milk
Pinch of cayenne pepper
Salt
Small bunches of watercress (to garnish)

❶ Remove fat from the bacon slices and chop the lean portion coarsely.

❷ Heat oil in a saucepan and sauté bacon, onion and garlic over medium heat, stirring.

❸ Pour in the white wine and chicken broth; mix well.

❹ Add the celery, potato and undrained crab meat. Bring to a boil and blend well.

❺ Reduce the heat and stir in tomato sauce, cream, milk and cayenne. Simmer for 15 minutes, stirring frequently.

❻ Add salt to taste. Float a small bunch of watercress over top.

• Makes 4 servings.

Chinese Bean Curd Soup

Preparation time: 10 min.
Cooking time: 30 min.

$^1/_3$ cup dried black mushrooms
3 cups (750 mL) chicken broth
1 cup bean curd, diced
$^1/_3$ cup barbecued pork (cha-siu), diced
$^1/_2$ seedless cucumber, diced
$^1/_2$ cup canned green peas
1 tbsp. light soy sauce
Salt
1 tbsp. Chinese cooking wine
1 tbsp. tapioca starch
4 tablespoons sliced green onion
  (scallion – to garnish)

❶ Soak the mushrooms in hot water for 2 to 3 hours or until soft. Drain and shred.

❷ Pour the chicken broth in a medium-sized saucepan and bring to a boil. Add the shredded mushrooms and remaining ingredients, except the cooking wine, tapioca starch, and green onion.

❸ Cook over medium-low heat for about 10 minutes or until the cucumber becomes transparent.

❹ Combine tapioca starch with cooking wine and pour into the saucepan, stirring. Simmer for 15 minutes.

❺ Sprinkle with sliced green onion.

● Makes 4 servings.

REMARK: *Above ingredients are available year-round in Chinese foodstores.*

Main Dishes

Seafood Crêpes (page 53)

Trou-aux-Biches Fisherman's Plate

Preparation time: 10 min.
Cooking time: 15 min.

¾ lb. (340 g) large shrimp, shelled (leave the tail shell attached)
¾ lb. (340 g) fresh scallops
Tabasco
3 tbsp. vegetable oil
2 cloves garlic, minced
1 small onion, finely chopped
¼ cup fresh coriander, minced
½ cup (125 mL) vermouth
½ cup (125 mL) tomato sauce
1 tbsp. ketchup
1 tsp. tapioca starch
⅓ cup (75 mL) water
Salt
White pepper

❶ Lightly sprinkle the shrimp and scallops with pepper. Drizzle with Tabasco. Mix thoroughly and set aside.

❷ In a large non-stick saucepan, heat oil over medium-high heat and sauté garlic and onion. Add shrimp and scallops and cook for 5 minutes, stirring. Sprinkle with 1 tablespoon of coriander and mix well.

❸ Pour in vermouth, tomato sauce and ketchup; blend well and cook for 3 minutes longer.

❹ Combine tapioca starch with water and pour over the shrimp and scallops. Lower the heat and cook, stirring until sauce thickens.

❺ Add salt to taste and sprinkle with remaining coriander.

❻ Arrange the seafood on a heated serving dish and pour sauce over seafood. Border with Island Papaya Fried Rice (see recipe next page) and serve immediately.

• Makes 4 servings.

Island Papaya Fried Rice

Preparation time: 18 min.
Cooking time: 35 min.

2 cups (360 g) long grain rice
1 1/2 tbsp. tomato sauce
2 3/4 cups (670 mL) chicken broth
1/4 tsp. cumin
1/4 tsp. curry powder
1 tbsp. finely chopped onion
1 clove garlic, finely chopped
1/4 cup (60 mL) vegetable oil
1 green or half-ripe papaya, peeled, seeded and sliced
3 tbsp. fresh coriander, minced
3 eggs, lightly beaten
Salt

❶ Put the rice in a large saucepan; rinse with water and drain well. Add tomato sauce, chicken broth, cumin, curry and 1 teaspoon of salt, blending well. Bring to a boil. Reduce heat to low, cover and cook **without stirring** for 20 minutes. Remove from heat and let stand, without stirring, for 10 minutes, covered. Set aside.

❷ In a large non-stick saucepan, sauté onion and garlic in 2 tablespoons of oil over high heat. Add the papaya slices and cook for 5 minutes, stirring. Sprinkle lightly with salt and 1 tablespoon of minced coriander. Mix well. Remove from saucepan and set aside.

❸ Lightly salt the beaten eggs. Pour into the saucepan and cook, stirring until crumbly. Remove from saucepan and set aside.

❹ In the same saucepan, heat 2 tablespoons of oil over medium heat and add the rice in small quantities. Stir until fluffy and well coated with oil.

❺ Return the papaya and scrambled eggs to the saucepan; season lightly with salt and mix thoroughly.

❻ Top with the remaining minced coriander and serve immediately.

● Makes 4 servings.

Chicken Curry with Eggplant and Kidney Beans

Preparation time: 10 min.
Cooking time: 30 min.

1 Italian eggplant, peeled and cut into small pieces
¼ cup (60 mL) vegetable oil
4 - 5 oz. (140 g) chicken breast halves, skinned and boned
1 chopped onion
1 tomato, peeled and quartered
1 - 10 oz. (284 mL) can white kidney beans, undrained
1 tbsp. curry powder
1 cup (250 mL) water
¼ tsp. cumin
Salt
8 cups cooked rice

❶ Soak the eggplant in salted water for about 2 hours and drain well.

❷ In a heavy non-stick skillet, heat 2 tablespoons of oil and sauté the chicken breasts, turning once, until browned. Keep warm.

❸ Sauté onion in 2 tablespoons of oil over medium heat in a large saucepan. Add the eggplant and tomato and cook for 5 minutes, stirring frequently. Stir in the undrained kidney beans and cook for a few minutes longer, blending well.

❹ Mix curry powder with water to make a smooth paste and pour mixture into the saucepan. Add cumin and bring to a boil.

❺ Lower the heat and return the chicken breasts to the saucepan. Cover and cook, stirring frequently, for 20 minutes longer or until the vegetables are tender and the sauce becomes thick and smooth. Add more water, if necessary. Season with salt.

❻ To serve, arrange the chicken breasts on a heated serving dish and pour curried eggplant sauce with kidney beans over each piece. Border with rice and serve immediately.

• Makes 4 servings.

Chayote-Beef Casserole

Preparation time: 20 min.
Cooking time: 60 min.

1 1/4 lb. (600 g) lean stewing beef, cut into cubes
4 tomatoes, peeled and cut into quarters
2 small onions, cut into pieces
1 tsp. thyme
Salt
1/4 tsp. black pepper
2 cups (500 mL) beef bouillon
2 chayotes, peeled, seeded and cut into large pieces
3 tbsp. vegetable oil
1 medium potato, peeled and cut into pieces
1 thinly sliced celery stalk
1 medium carrot, sliced
1/2 tsp. oregano
1/2 tsp. dried parsley flakes
1/2 cup (125 mL) tomato sauce
1/4 cup (60 mL) red Bordeaux (optional)

❶ Combine beef, tomatoes, pieces of one onion, thyme, 1/2 teaspoon of salt, pepper and beef bouillon in a pressure cooker. Cover and cook over medium heat for 25 minutes after pot whistles.

❷ Drop the pressure of the cooker, then remove the cover and add the chayotes. Close and cook for 5 minutes longer after pot whistles.

❸ When done, remove the meat and the chayotes with a slotted spoon and set the sauce aside.

❹ Pour oil in a large Dutch oven and sauté remaining onion over medium heat. Add beef and chayotes and sauté for about 2 minutes, stirring. Pour 1 3/4 cups (420 mL) of the reserved sauce, then add remaining ingredients.

❺ Mix well and bring to a boil. Lower the heat; cover and cook, stirring frequently, for about 20 minutes or until the vegetables are tender. Add salt to taste.

❻ Serve with rice or French bread.

● Makes 4 servings.

Chayote-Beef Casserole

In the Caribbean, the chayote is widely known as "christophine" whereas in Mauritius and Reunion Island, it is known as "chouchou". In India, it is called "chouchoute" and in other areas of the world, "brionne" and "mirliton".

Fisherman's Cauliflower

Preparation time: 10 min.
Cooking time: 35 min.

2 tbsp. dried ground shrimp**
3 tbsp. vegetable oil
2 tbsp. onion, chopped coarsely
2 cloves garlic, minced
¾ lb. (340 g) lean ground beef
6 cups cauliflower flowerets
½ cup (125 mL) dry white wine
2 cups (500 mL) chicken broth
4 eggs, lightly beaten
⅓ cup (75 mL) light cream
2 tbsp. tapioca starch
½ cup (125 mL) water
Salt
¼ cup fresh coriander, minced

** *Dried shrimp is available year-round in Chinese foodstores in packaged form. Using a food processor, grind finely.*

❶ In a large saucepan, heat 3 tablespoons of oil over medium heat. Sauté together the onion, garlic and ground shrimp. Add ground beef and cook for about 5 minutes, stirring constantly, until browned.

❷ Toss in cauliflower and mix well. Cover and cook for about 5 minutes, stirring frequently, until slightly translucent. Pour in wine and chicken broth and mix well. Cover and cook until tender, stirring frequently.

❸ Blend in beaten eggs and cream. Combine tapioca starch with water, then pour into the saucepan. Cook over low heat, stirring until sauce thickens. Add salt to taste.

❹ Top with a sprinkling of chopped coriander and serve.

● Makes 4 servings.

Chinese Spare-Ribs

Preparation time: 10 min.
Cooking time: 30 min.

2 lb. (1 kg) pork spare-ribs [flank] cut into serving pieces
Light soy sauce
3 1/2 tbsp. tapioca starch
2 cloves garlic, minced
3 tbsp. salted black beans (soybeans)

REMARK: *The salted black beans (soya beans), tapioca starch and soy sauce are available year-round in Chinese foodstores. Salted black beans are fermented and should always be washed before using.*

❶ In a large heatproof bowl, place ribs and sprinkle generously with soy sauce. Sprinkle with tapioca starch, garlic and black beans. Mix together until ribs are well coated with the mixture.

❷ Place bowl in top of double boiler and steam over simmering water for 25 minutes. Blend thoroughly and steam for 5 minutes longer.

❸ The ribs will be deliciously flavored. Serve with rice and Chinese Sautéed Vegetables (see recipe next page).

● Makes 4 servings.

Chinese Sautéed Vegetables

Preparation time: 15 min.
Cooking time: 15 min.

1 clove garlic, minced
1 medium onion, quartered and sliced
2 tbsp. vegetable oil
3 bok-choy stalks, stripped into julienne
2 cups broccoli flowerets
1 - 8 oz. (227 mL) can bamboo shoots, shredded and drained
2 tsp. light soy sauce
2 tsp. oyster sauce
1 tbsp. sherry
1 tbsp. tapioca starch
1 cup (250 mL) water
Salt

❶ In a large wok, sauté garlic and onion in 2 tablespoons of oil over high heat.

❷ Add vegetables and stir-fry for about 5 minutes until fork-tender. Lower the heat.

❸ Sprinkle with soy sauce, oyster sauce and sherry. Combine tapioca starch with water; blend well and pour into the wok. Cook, stirring until sauce thickens.

❹ Add salt to taste and serve with the spare-ribs (previous recipe).

• Makes 4 servings.

Oriental Style Sliced Beef

Preparation time: 20 min.
Cooking time: 25 min.

1 cup dried black mushrooms
1 lb. (500 g) sirloin, cut into small, thin slices
2 tbsp. mushroom soy sauce
1 tsp. garlic powder
$1/4$ tsp. ground ginger
2 tbsp. tapioca starch
$1/2$ cup (125 mL) vegetable oil
3 cups snow peas (remove tips)
1 clove garlic, minced
1 tbsp. chopped fresh ginger
2 - 8 oz. (227 mL) cans shredded bamboo shoots, drained
$1/4$ cup (60 mL) sherry
2 abalones, thinly sliced
1 tbsp. oyster sauce
1 cup (250 mL) water
1 tbsp. light soy sauce
Salt

Oriental Style Sliced Beef (cont'd)

❶ Soak mushrooms in hot water for 1 or 2 hours until softened. Drain and shred. Set aside.

❷ Drizzle the beef slices with mushroom soy sauce. Sprinkle with garlic powder, ground ginger and 1½ tablespoons of tapioca starch. Mix together to coat well.

❸ In a large non-stick wok, heat 3 tablespoons of oil over high heat and stir-fry the beef slices for 4 minutes. Remove from wok and keep warm.

❹ Heat 2 tablespoons of oil in the same wok and stir-fry snow peas until tender. Remove from wok and keep warm.

❺ In the same wok, heat 2 tablespoons of oil over medium-high heat and sauté garlic and ginger. Add bamboo shoots and mushrooms and cook for 3 minutes, stirring. Pour in sherry and blend well.

❻ Add the abalones and oyster sauce and cook for 1 minute, stirring constantly. Combine remaining tapioca starch with water and 1 tablespoon of light soy sauce, then pour into the wok. Cook, stirring continuously, until sauce thickens. Return the beef slices and the snow peas to the wok and mix thoroughly.

❼ Add salt to taste. Serve with rice.

● Makes 4 servings.

Seafood Crêpes

Preparation time: 25 min.
Cooking time: 25 min.

12 cooked crêpes (see recipe "Morne Brabant Crêpes with Chicken and Chayote", page 54)
36 cooked fresh asparagus
1 tbsp. butter
1 1/2 cups large fresh shelled and deveined shrimp
1 1/2 cups fresh scallops
1 - 4 oz. (112 g) can crab meat, drained
1/3 cup (50 g) all-purpose flour
1 1/2 cups (375 mL) chicken broth
1/2 cup (125 mL) milk
2 tsp. Worcestershire sauce
1/3 cup (30 g) grated mild cheddar cheese
1/2 cup (125 mL) sour cream
1/4 cup (60 mL) whipping cream
Pinch of white pepper
1/4 tsp. salt
Paprika

❶ Heat butter in a non-stick skillet over high heat until sizzling. Sauté shrimp and scallops. Remove from skillet and keep warm.

❷ Sauté crab meat in the leftover butter, stirring. Sprinkle flour over crab meat and mix well. Gradually add the chicken broth and stir until well blended.

❸ Stir in milk, Worcestershire sauce, grated cheese, sour cream, whipping cream, pepper and salt. Cook over low heat, stirring, until mixture thickens.

❹ Arrange asparagus, scallops and shrimp on crêpes and spoon 1/4 cup (60 mL) of sauce over each; fold crêpes over.

❺ Place in greased shallow baking pan and pour remaining sauce over filled crêpes. Cover with aluminum foil. Heat in a preheated 350°F (175°C) oven for 15 minutes.

❻ Sprinkle lightly with paprika and serve.

● Makes 4 servings.

See photograph on page 43.

Morne Brabant Crêpes with Chicken and Chayote

Preparation time: 35 min.
Cooking time: 50 min.

BATTER:

3 eggs
Pinch of salt
1 cup (140 g) all-purpose flour
1 1/3 cups (325 mL) milk
1/4 cup (60 mL) melted butter

❶ In a medium mixing bowl, beat eggs and salt at a slow speed, using an electric mixer. Add flour gradually and alternately with milk.

❷ Fold in melted butter.

❸ Refrigerate at least one hour before using.

❹ Place a non-stick skillet over medium heat and brush with butter. Pour in 1/4 cup (60 mL) of batter. Lift and tilt the skillet in a circular motion in order to spread batter over the bottom of the skillet. Cook until light golden brown; carefully turn the crêpe with a plastic spatula and cook the other side. There is no need to grease the pan for cooking remaining batter.

• Makes 14 crêpes.

REMARK: Crêpes can be stored in the refrigerator for about 3 days, when properly secured in foil or plastic wrap, and up to 2 months in the freezer. Use wax paper to separate them and freezer bags or freezer containers for storage in the freezer.

Morne Brabant Crêpes with Chicken and Chayote (cont'd)

FILLING:

2 cloves garlic, finely chopped
1/4 cup (60 mL) vegetable oil
4 chayotes, peeled, seeded and sliced
2 chicken breasts, cut into small pieces
2 cups (500 mL) chicken broth
1/2 cup (125 mL) sour cream
1/2 cup (125 mL) whipping cream
3 1/2 tbsp. flour
1 cup (250 mL) milk
1 tsp. ketchup
1/4 tsp. curry powder
Salt
White pepper
Cayenne pepper

❶ Sauté 1 chopped clove of garlic in 2 tablespoons of oil in a saucepan. Add the sliced chayotes; stir, cover and cook over medium heat for about 10 minutes, stirring frequently, until tender.

❷ Remove from saucepan and keep warm.

❸ Lightly sprinkle the chicken with salt and white pepper.

❹ In the same saucepan, add 2 tablespoons of oil and sauté remaining chopped garlic over medium-high heat; add the chicken and cook for a few minutes, stirring constantly, until done. Remove from pan and keep warm.

❺ Pour the chicken broth, sour cream and whipping cream into the saucepan and blend well.

❻ Combine flour, milk, ketchup and curry. Pour into the saucepan and cook over low heat, stirring until thickened. Season lightly with salt. Strain sauce, if necessary.

❼ Fill each crêpe with chicken and chayotes. Pour some sauce over and fold crêpe.

❽ Arrange crêpes on a heated serving dish and garnish with remaining slices of chayotes. Lightly sprinkle with cayenne and serve immediately.

● Makes 4 servings.

Touessrok Sliced Pork Legs

Preparation time: 12 min.
Cooking time: 25 min.

4 - 5 oz. (140 g) sliced pork legs
Light soy sauce
1/3 cup (75 mL) vegetable oil
2 cloves garlic, minced
1 - 8 oz. (227 mL) can pineapple chunks, drained
1 tbsp. tapioca starch
1 cup (250 mL) pineapple juice
1/4 cup (60 mL) sherry
1/2 cup (125 mL) water
Dash of Tabasco
Cooked carrot sticks (to garnish)
Black pepper
Salt

❶ Drizzle the pork with some soy sauce and sprinkle lightly with pepper.

❷ Heat 2 tablespoons of oil over high heat in a heavy non-stick skillet and sauté the slices of pork leg, one at a time, until browned on both sides. Add more oil, if necessary, for cooking the remaining pork legs. Drain and keep warm.

❸ In another skillet, sauté garlic in 1 tablespoon of oil over medium heat. Add the drained pineapple chunks, then sprinkle tapioca starch over the pineapple. Mix thoroughly. Pour in the pineapple juice, sherry and water. Season with salt and Tabasco. Cook over medium heat, stirring constantly, until sauce thickens.

❹ Arrange the pork on a heated serving dish and pour sauce with the pineapple chunks over the pork. Garnish with carrot sticks.

• Makes 4 servings.

Curried Fish Steaks

Preparation time: 10 min.
Cooking time: 45 min.

4 - 1½-inch (3.5-cm) thick fresh fish steaks
Vegetable oil
2 tbsp. tapioca starch
2 cups (500 mL) water
2 tbsp. curry powder
½ tsp. cumin
2 tsp. turmeric
2 tbsp. finely chopped onion
1 clove garlic, finely chopped
Salt

❶ Lightly salt the fish steaks.

❷ Fry in hot oil at 375°F (190°C) for 5 to 7 minutes, turning once. Remove with a slotted spoon and drain well on paper towels. Set aside.

❸ Combine the tapioca starch, water, curry powder, cumin and turmeric, blending well to make a smooth paste.

❹ Sauté onion and garlic in 2 tablespoons of oil over medium heat in a large saucepan. Stir in the curry mixture. Bring to a boil; lower the heat, then put in the fish steaks. Cook for 30 minutes longer over low heat, frequently spooning sauce over the steaks. Turn the steaks once after 15 minutes. Add salt to taste.

❺ Place the steaks on a heated serving platter and pour curried sauce over the steaks. Spoon fluffy rice into an even border around the fish steaks and serve immediately.

● Makes 4 servings.

Poached Salmon with Chestnut Sauce

Preparation time: 18 min.
Cooking time: 75 min.

1 - 1¾ lb. (800 g) fresh pink salmon
Black pepper
Cooked carrot sticks (to garnish)

COURT-BOUILLON:

4 cups (1 litre) chicken broth
1 celery stalk, sliced
2 cloves garlic, minced
1 onion, sliced
¼ cup (60 mL) dry white wine
3 tbsp. tomato sauce
¼ tsp. paprika
¼ tsp. nutmeg
½ tsp. thyme
2 black peppercorns
2 tsp. salt

❶ Slice the salmon into 1½-inch (3.5-cm) steaks and lightly sprinkle with pepper.

To prepare the court-bouillon:

❷ In a large saucepan, bring the chicken broth to a boil. Add the remaining ingredients and simmer for 40 minutes.

❸ Poach the steaks for 12 minutes; drain and keep warm.

Poached Salmon with Chestnut Sauce   (cont'd)

CHESTNUT SAUCE:

1 tbsp. butter
1 tbsp. flour
¼ cup (60 mL) sherry
¼ cup (60 mL) light cream
3 tbsp. chestnut purée
1 tbsp. honey
Salt

❹ Melt butter in a skillet over medium heat; add flour and blend well.

❺ Stir in 2 cups (500 mL) of the court-bouillon, sherry and cream. Fold in chestnut purée and honey.

❻ Bring to a boil, then reduce the heat and simmer for 15 minutes, stirring frequently. Add salt to taste.

❼ Arrange steak on a heated serving dish and pour sauce over it. Garnish with cooked carrot sticks and serve immediately.

● Makes 4 servings.

Veal Scallops with Prunes

Preparation time: 8 min.
Cooking time: 30 min.

Veal Scallops with Prunes (cont'd)

4 - 5 oz. (140 g) veal scallops
   or 12 cutlets
2 dozen pitted prunes
1 cup (250 mL) water
1 cup (250 mL) red wine
1/4 cup (115 g) butter
1 tbsp. minced green onion (scallion)
1 tbsp. tapioca starch
2 tbsp. honey
Cooked carrot sticks (to garnish)
Salt
Black pepper

❶ Pound the scallops with a meat mallet. Lightly sprinkle with salt and pepper. Set aside.

❷ Place the prunes in a medium-sized saucepan. Pour in water and 1/2 cup (125 mL) of wine. Season lightly with salt. Bring to a boil; reduce the heat and simmer for 10 minutes, stirring occasionally.

❸ Meanwhile, in a skillet, brown 2 or 3 scallops on both sides in 2 tablespoons of butter over high heat. Add some butter, if necessary, for browning remaining scallops. Keep warm.

❹ In the same skillet, sauté the minced green onion in leftover butter and stir in the remaining wine. Combine tapioca starch with 1/4 cup (60 mL) of prune cooking liquid, then pour into the skillet. Blend in honey and season lightly with salt.

❺ Add the cooked prunes together with the remaining prune cooking liquid and stir until well blended. Simmer until sauce thickens.

❻ Remove the prunes with a slotted spoon and strain the liquid through a sieve.

❼ To serve, spoon sauce over the scallops. Garnish with some cooked prunes and a few carrot sticks.

● Makes 4 servings.

Butterfly Pork Chops with Leek

Preparation time: 13 min.
Cooking time: 17 min.

4 - 5 oz. (140 g) butterfly pork chops
3 tbsp. vegetable oil
2 cloves garlic, chopped
1 1/2 cups sliced white leeks
1/3 cup (75 mL) sherry
1 cup (250 mL) pineapple juice
Pinch of cayenne pepper
1 tbsp. tapioca starch
Salt
White pepper
Croutons
Zucchini or eggplant fritters

❶ Lightly sprinkle pork chops with salt and pepper.

❷ Heat 3 tablespoons of oil in a skillet over high heat and brown the pork chops on both sides. Remove from pan and keep warm.

❸ In the same skillet, sauté garlic in the leftover oil, then add the leeks. Cook, stirring continuously, for a few minutes until leeks are tender. Pour in the sherry and 1/2 cup (125mL) of pineapple juice. Mix well.

❹ Add cayenne. Combine tapioca starch with the remaining pineapple juice and pour into the skillet. Cook over low heat, stirring constantly until sauce thickens. Add salt to taste.

❺ Arrange the pork chops on a heated serving platter and spoon leek sauce over chops. Serve with croutons and vegetable fritters such as eggplant or zucchini.

● Makes 4 servings.

Sole Fillets with Shrimp-Tomato Sauce

Preparation time: 10 min.
Cooking time: 30 min.

4 sole fillets
1 1/2 cups (375 mL) milk
1/2 cup (125 mL) white wine
1/4 cup (60 g) butter
1 chopped clove garlic
1 tbsp. finely chopped onion
2 - 4 oz. (113 g) cans shrimp (cocktail), drained
1/4 cup (60 mL) tomato sauce
Pinch of oregano
Pinch of savory
1 tbsp. tapioca starch
Salt
White pepper
Cooked carrot sticks
Cooked broccoli flowerets
Parsley sprigs (to garnish)

❶ Place the fish fillets in a greased shallow heatproof dish. Drizzle with 1/2 cup (125 mL) of milk and 1/4 cup (60 mL) of white wine. Lightly sprinkle with salt and pepper.

❷ Dot the fillets with 3 tablespoons of butter. Cover with aluminum foil and bake in a preheated 375°F (190°C) oven for 20 minutes. Remove the aluminum foil and pour the juice into a bowl; set aside. Keep the fillets warm.

❸ In a skillet, sauté garlic and onion in 1 tablespoon of butter over medium-high heat. Add the drained shrimp and cook for a few minutes, stirring. Stir in remaining white wine.

❹ Add tomato sauce, the reserved juice, oregano and savory. Combine the tapioca starch with remaining milk and stir into the mixture until well blended.

❺ Bring to a boil; reduce the heat and cook until sauce thickens. Add salt to taste.

❻ Place the fillets on a heated serving platter and top with the shrimp-tomato sauce. Garnish with parsley sprigs and serve with cooked carrot sticks and broccoli flowerets.

● Makes 4 servings.

Sole Fillets with Shrimp-Tomato Sauce

Sweet and Sour Beef Liver with Radishes

Preparation time: 20 min.
Cooking time: 30 min.

³/₄ lb. (340 g) radishes (remove ends)
4 slices 5.5 oz. (150 g) beef liver, skinned
¹/₃ cup (75 mL) vegetable oil
1 tbsp. chopped onion
¹/₃ cup (75 mL) wine vinegar
2 tbsp. honey
Dash of Tabasco
¹/₃ cup (75 mL) pineapple juice
1¹/₄ tbsp. tapioca starch
¹/₂ cup (125 mL) water
Salt
Black pepper
A few radishes (to garnish)

Sweet and Sour Beef Liver with Radishes (cont'd)

❶ Using a food processor, thinly slice the radishes.

❷ Season the liver with salt and pepper.

❸ Heat 3 tablespoons of oil in a heavy non-stick skillet and sauté liver over high heat until browned. Keep warm.

❹ In a medium saucepan, sauté onion in 3 tablespoons of oil over medium heat and add the sliced radishes. Cook, stirring frequently, for 5 minutes or until slightly transparent.

❺ Pour in wine vinegar; blend in honey and Tabasco.

❻ Lower the heat and cook 5 minutes longer, stirring until the radishes are tender.

❼ Combine pineapple juice, tapioca starch and water. Pour mixture into the saucepan and cook, stirring until thickened.

❽ Add salt to taste.

❾ Arrange the liver on a heated serving dish. Pour sweet and sour sauce with radishes over the meat. Garnish with raw radishes.

● Makes 4 servings.

Chayote Flan

Preparation time: 38 min.
(including the crust)
Cooking time: 50 min.
(including the crust)

1 flan crust (see recipe "Zucchini-Shrimp Quiche", page 83)
1 1/2 tbsp. butter
2 medium chayotes, peeled, seeded and cut into julienne strips
1/3 cup (30 g) cornstarch
1/2 cup (125 mL) milk
3 eggs, beaten
1/4 cup (60 mL) whipping cream
1 cup (100 g) grated mild cheddar cheese
Dash of white pepper
Salt
Sprigs of parsley (to garnish)

❶ Prepare a crust as directed in recipe "Zucchini-Shrimp Quiche" but using a 9 x 1 1/4-inch (23 x 3-cm) removable-bottom fluted pie tin.

❷ Heat butter in a skillet over medium heat until bubbly. Add the chayotes and cook for 5 to 10 minutes, stirring until tender and translucent. Season lightly with salt.

❸ Spread the chayotes in the crust and set aside.

❹ Combine cornstarch with milk; add eggs, cream, 1/3 cup (30 g) of grated cheese, pepper and 1/4 teaspoon of salt, blending well. Pour mixture into the crust over the chayotes and sprinkle with remaining grated cheese.

❺ Bake in a preheated 375°F (190°C) oven for 25 to 30 minutes or until a wooden pick inserted near the center comes out clean.

❻ Garnish with parsley sprigs and serve with Artichoke-Corn Salad, page 34.

● Makes 4 servings.

REMARK: *When using a pie tin of only 1-inch height, substitute the medium chayotes for 2 small ones.*

Pirate's Beef Liver with Pepper

Preparation time: 15 min.
Cooking time: 25 min.

4 - 5 oz. (130 g) slices beef liver, skinned
Light soy sauce
1/4 tsp. cayenne pepper
1 small onion, finely chopped
2 cloves garlic, minced
1/4 cup (60 mL) vegetable oil
1 green pepper, seeded and shredded
1 red pepper, seeded and shredded
1/3 cup (75 mL) cider
1 1/2 tsp. tapioca starch
1 cup (250 mL) exotic fruit-juice mix
1/4 tsp. garlic powder
Black pepper
Salt
1/4 cup chopped fresh coriander

*P*irate's Beef Liver with Pepper (cont'd)

❶ Sprinkle the liver lightly with black pepper, soy sauce, cayenne, onion and garlic. Mix together.

❷ Heat 2 tablespoons of oil over high heat in a heavy non-stick skillet and sauté liver until browned. Remove from skillet and keep warm.

❸ In another skillet, sauté shredded green and red peppers in 2 tablespoons of oil over high heat, stirring frequently, until crisp-tender. Lower the heat and drizzle with cider. Cook for 2 minutes longer, stirring until tender.

❹ Combine tapioca starch with 1 cup (250 mL) of exotic fruit juice and pour mixture over the shredded peppers. Add garlic powder. Cook over low heat, mixing occasionally, until sauce thickens. Add salt to taste.

❺ Place the beef liver on a heated serving dish and arrange the peppers on one side. Pour sauce over the liver and top with a sprinkling of chopped fresh coriander. Remaining peppers and sauce may be offered in a sauceboat.

● Makes 4 servings.

---

*S*eafood with Papaya

Preparation time: 13 min.
Cooking time: 23 min.

¾ lb. (340 g) fresh scampi, shelled and deveined (leave the tail shell attached)
½ lb. (225 g) fresh scallops
1 clove garlic, minced
1 tsp. fresh ginger, chopped
1 tsp. Tabasco
¼ cup (60 mL) vegetable oil
¼ cup minced green onion (scallion)
1 half-ripe papaya, peeled, seeded and sliced
2 tbsp. tomato sauce
½ cup (125 mL) water
2 tbsp. grapefruit juice
½ cup (125 mL) pineapple juice
2 tbsp. sherry
1 tbsp. tapioca starch
2 tsp. ketchup
Salt
White pepper

Seafood with Papaya *(cont'd)*

❶ Sprinkle scampi and scallops with garlic, ginger, Tabasco, salt and pepper. Mix together and set aside.

❷ Heat 2 tablespoons of oil in a large non-stick saucepan and sauté half a tablespoon of green onion over high heat. Add papaya and cook for 4 to 5 minutes, stirring frequently, until tender. Remove from saucepan and keep warm.

❸ Heat the remaining 2 tablespoons of oil in the same saucepan and sauté the seafood over high heat for 5 minutes. Sprinkle with 1 tablespoon of green onion. Remove from saucepan and keep warm. Leave the juices in the saucepan.

❹ Combine the tomato sauce, water, grapefruit juice, pineapple juice, sherry, tapioca starch and ketchup and pour into the saucepan. Cook over low-medium heat, stirring until thickened. Add salt to taste and sprinkle with 1 tablespoon of green onion. Blend thoroughly.

❺ Arrange the seafood and papaya on a heated platter and pour sauce over all. Surround with tomato rice (see recipe next page) and sprinkle with remaining green onion. Serve immediately.

● Makes 4 servings.

An exotic and attractive dish!

Tomato Rice

Preparation time: 8 min.
Cooking time: 12 min.

3 tbsp. vegetable oil
1 tbsp. finely chopped onion
1 clove garlic, minced
2 tomatoes, peeled and cut into medium pieces
1 tbsp. minced green onion (scallion)
2 cups cooked long grain rice
Salt

❶ Heat 1 tablespoon of oil in a skillet and sauté onion and garlic over high heat.

❷ Add tomatoes and cook for 3 to 5 minutes, stirring. Season lightly with salt. Remove from skillet with a slotted spoon and set aside.

❸ In a large saucepan, heat the remaining 2 tablespoons of oil and sauté green onion over medium heat. Add the cooked rice in small quantities and sprinkle lightly with salt. Stir until rice is coated with oil. Add tomatoes and mix well.

● Makes 4 servings.

Chinese Fried Rice

Preparation time: 25 min.
Cooking time: 18 min.

Chinese Fried Rice *(cont'd)*

2 cups (360 g) long grain rice
2 1/2 cups (625 mL) chicken broth
1 tsp. salt
3 eggs
1/4 cup (60 mL) vegetable oil
1/3 cup minced green onion (scallion)
2 cups diced barbecued pork (cha-siu)
2 carrots, diced
1 - 10 oz. (284 mL) can green peas, drained
2 tbsp. Chinese cooking wine (optional)
1 1/2 tbsp. light soy sauce

❶ Put the rice in a medium-sized saucepan; rinse with water and drain well. Add chicken broth and season with salt. Mix well and bring to a boil.

❷ Reduce heat to low; cover and cook for 20 minutes, **without stirring**. Remove from heat and let stand (without stirring) for 10 minutes, covered.

❸ Meanwhile, lightly beat eggs together with a pinch of salt. Set aside.

❹ Heat 2 tablespoons of oil in a large non-stick wok and sauté 1 tablespoon of green onion over high heat. Throw in the diced barbecued pork and cook, stirring, for a few minutes.

❺ Add carrots and peas; cook for 3 minutes, stirring. Add cooking wine; mix, then add the beaten eggs. Sprinkle with 2 tablespoons of green onion and cook, stirring vigorously, until eggs become crumbly. Remove mixture from wok and keep warm.

❻ In the same wok, heat the remaining 2 tablespoons of oil over high heat and add the rice in small quantities. Mix well and stir in the egg mixture.

❼ Lower the heat and drizzle with 1 1/2 tablespoons of soy sauce. Mix thoroughly and sprinkle the remaining green onion on top.

● Makes 4 servings.

REMARK: This glamorous and deliciously flavored rice dish will always have a place in a sumptuous buffet. It is easily prepared and makes a nice treat for guests.

Salted Cod Flan

Preparation time: 45 min.
(including the crust)
Cooking time: 32 min.
(including the crust)

1 flan crust (see recipe "Zucchini-Shrimp Quiche", page 83)
¾ lb. (340 g) salted cod fillet
1 cup (250 mL) milk
2 tbsp. whipping cream
¼ tsp. cayenne pepper
¾ cup (75 g) grated mild cheddar cheese
3 eggs, beaten
3 tbsp. tapioca starch
2 cherry tomatoes, sliced
Dash of white pepper
Sprigs of parsley (to garnish)

❶ Soak the cod in plenty of water overnight.

❷ Prepare a flan crust as directed in recipe "Zucchini-Shrimp Quiche" but use a 9-inch (23-cm) diameter and 1¼-inch (3-cm) high fluted pie tin with a removable bottom. Set aside.

❸ Drain the cod fillet and flake slowly. If it is not a fillet, carefully remove all the bones.

❹ Pour the milk in a saucepan and bring to a boil. Toss in the fish. Cook over medium heat for 2 to 3 minutes, stirring. Blend in pepper, cream, cayenne and ⅓ cup (35 g) of grated cheese. Remove from heat.

❺ Beat eggs and tapioca starch with a whisk and blend into the milk-cod mixture.

❻ Pour into the prepared crust and top with sliced cherry tomatoes. Sprinkle with remaining grated cheese and bake in a preheated 375°F (190°C) oven for 25 to 30 minutes or until a wooden pick inserted in the center comes out clean.

❼ To serve, remove the ring around the flan and place on a serving platter. Garnish with sprigs of parsley.

● Makes 4 to 6 servings.

REMARK: *If the pie tin is only 1 inch (2.5 cm) high, put ½ lb. (230 g) of cod fillet instead of ¾ lb. (340 g).*

Salted Cod Flan

Marylin's Pineapple Chicken

Preparation time: 20 min.
Cooking time: 20 min.

4 - 5 oz. (140 g) chicken breast halves, skinned and boned
1/2 cup (125 mL) cider
Garlic powder
1 tsp. fresh ginger, finely chopped
1 small onion, finely chopped
2 tbsp. vegetable oil
1 - 14 oz. (398 mL) can pineapple chunks,
    drained (reserve 1 cup [250 mL] juice)
1/2 cup (125 mL) chicken broth
1 1/2 tbsp. tapioca starch
1 tbsp. honey
1 tbsp. cayenne pepper
Cooked carrot sticks (to garnish)
Pinch white pepper
Salt

Marylin's Pineapple Chicken   (cont'd)

❶ Pound chicken breasts with a meat mallet. Drizzle with 2 tablespoons of cider; sprinkle lightly with garlic powder, pepper and salt.

❷ Sauté ginger and onion in 2 tablespoons of oil in a large non-stick skillet over medium heat. Sauté chicken, turning once, until golden brown. Keep warm.

❸ Stir remaining cider in the skillet drippings and add the drained pineapple pieces. Cook for 3 minutes over medium heat, stirring. Add the chicken broth. Combine tapioca starch with the reserved pineapple juice and pour into the skillet.

❹ Return the chicken breasts to the skillet and mix together well. Cook for 3 minutes longer, stirring until sauce thickens. Blend in honey and add salt to taste.

❺ Place chicken on a heated serving dish. Remove pineapples with a slotted spoon and place on one side of the dish. Spoon sauce over the chicken and sprinkle lightly with cayenne. Garnish with cooked carrot sticks.

● Makes 4 servings.

Chinese Steamed Fresh Fish

Preparation time: 10 min.
Cooking time: 25 min.

1 - 1³/₄ lb. (800 g) whole fresh red snapper, scaled and cleaned
2 tbsp. sesame oil
2 tbsp. light soy sauce
2 tbsp. fish sauce
1 tsp. minced fresh ginger
2 cloves garlic, chopped
4 tbsp. minced fresh coriander

❶ Make 3 shallow slits diagonally every 1¹/₂ inch (3.5 cm) on each side of the fish.

❷ In a small mixing bowl, combine sesame oil, 1 tablespoon of soy sauce and fish sauce. Brush the fish outside and inside with the oil mixture.

❸ Combine ginger and garlic and insert a pinch of the mixture into the slits as well as inside the fish. Arrange fish on a heatproof oval dish and brush with the remaining sesame oil mixture. Sprinkle with 2 tablespoons of minced coriander.

❹ Place the dish in a large double boiler and steam the fish over simmering water for 20 to 25 minutes or until it flakes easily with a fork.

❺ Spoon dish juices over the fish and drizzle with remaining soy sauce. Garnish with remaining coriander and serve immediately.

● Makes 4 servings.

Oriental Fish with Noodles and Vegetables

Preparation time: 25 min.
Cooking time: 30 min.

Noodles:

12 oz. (340 g) noodles
3 tbsp. vegetable oil
1 tbsp. light soy sauce
2 tbsp. chopped fresh coriander
Salt

Fish:

4 - 5 oz. (140 g) fish fillets
  (bluefish, cod)
2 tbsp. mushroom soy sauce
1 tbsp. fish sauce
2 tbsp. sesame oil
1 clove garlic, minced
1 tbsp. chopped fresh ginger
2 tbsp. chopped fresh coriander

Vegetables:

1 clove garlic, minced
3 tbsp. vegetable oil
3 carrots, sliced
1 bok-choy (stalks only), stripped into
  julienne
2 cups broccoli flowerets
3 tbsp. tapioca starch
1 tbsp. Chinese cooking wine
2 cups (500 mL) fish stock or chicken
  broth
1 tbsp. light soy sauce
1 tbsp. oyster sauce (optional)
¼ cup chopped fresh coriander
Salt

To prepare the noodles:

❶ Cook the noodles in slightly salted boiling water (do not add salt if the noodles have already been salted) for 2 to 3 minutes or until tender. Drain. Rinse quickly under cold water and drain well.

❷ Heat oil over medium heat in a large wok. Add the noodles in small quantities and sprinkle with soy sauce and coriander. Cook for a few minutes, stirring until noodles are coated with oil. Place in a large oval heatproof serving platter and keep warm.

To prepare the fish:

❸ Drizzle the fish fillets with soy sauce, fish sauce and sesame oil. Sprinkle with garlic, ginger and coriander. Mix together.

❹ Arrange the fillets on a heatproof dish and place in a large steamer. Steam the fish over boiling water, without turning, for 7 to 10 minutes or until fish flakes easily with a fork (steam only 2 at a time, if necessary). Arrange the fillets over the noodles and spoon some of the juice over the fish. Keep warm.

Oriental Fish with Noodles and Vegetables (cont'd)

To prepare the vegetables:

❺ In the wok, sauté garlic in oil over high heat and stir-fry the vegetables for 3 to 4 minutes or until crisp-tender.

❻ Set the heat at medium-high. Combine tapioca starch, wine, fish stock or chicken broth, soy sauce and oyster sauce and pour mixture over the vegetables. Cook, stirring until sauce thickens. Add salt to taste. Arrange vegetables over the noodles.

❼ Sprinkle with coriander and serve immediately.

● Makes 4 servings.

REMARK: This succulent dish is perfect for a buffet. Since the noodles, the fish and the vegetables are prepared and can be served separately, your guests can help themselves according to their taste. It can be easily prepared for any number of guests.

Chicken in Mango Sauce

Preparation time: 12 min.
Cooking time: 20 min.

1 small ripe mango, peeled and sliced
$1/3$ cup (75 mL) pineapple juice
4 - 5 oz. (140 g) chicken breast halves, skinned and boned
$1/2$ cup (125 mL) cider
1 tsp. ground ginger
1 tsp. garlic powder
3 tbsp. vegetable oil
1 clove garlic, finely chopped
1 tsp. fresh finely chopped ginger
Dash of Tabasco
Cooked carrot sticks
2 large ripe mangoes, peeled and sliced
Salt
White pepper
Watercress (to garnish)

❶ Place the slices of the small mango together with the pineapple juice in a blender and process until well puréed.

❷ Pound chicken breasts with a meat mallet and lightly sprinkle with 2 tablespoons of cider, ground ginger, garlic powder, salt and pepper. Mix well.

❸ Heat 2 tablespoons of oil over medium-high heat in a large heavy non-stick skillet. Sauté chicken breasts until browned. Keep warm.

❹ In another skillet, sauté garlic and ginger in remaining 1 tablespoon of oil over medium heat. Add the remaining cider, Tabasco and a pinch of white pepper, stirring until well blended. Fold in the puréed mango and simmer for 5 minutes.

❺ Add salt to taste.

❻ Pour the mango sauce over the chicken on a heated dish and arrange mango slices and carrot sticks around chicken. Garnish with watercress and serve immediately.

● Makes 4 servings.

Chicken in Mango Sauce

Sun Fried Rice

Preparation time: 15 min.
Cooking time: 30 min.

RICE:

2 cups (360 g) long grain rice
3 cups (750 mL) chicken broth
3 tbsp. dry white wine
2 cloves garlic, minced
¼ tsp. turmeric
¼ tsp. curry powder
¼ tsp. cumin
2 tsp. salt

❶ Put rice in a medium-sized saucepan. Rinse with cold water and drain well. Add remaining ingredients and blend thoroughly. Bring to a boil, then reduce heat to low. Cover and cook for 20 minutes **without stirring**. Remove from heat and let stand, covered, for 10 minutes, again without stirring.

❷ Meantime, prepare the vegetables:

Sun Fried Rice (cont'd)

VEGETABLES:

1 tbsp. finely chopped onion
1 clove garlic, minced
3 tbsp. vegetable oil
1 green pepper, seeded and shredded
1 red pepper, seeded and shredded
1 tomato, chopped coarsely
Salt

❸ In a large saucepan, sauté onion and garlic over medium heat in 1 tablespoon of oil.

❹ Toss in the shredded green and red peppers and the tomato. Cook, stirring continuously, until fork-tender. Season lightly with salt. Remove vegetables from saucepan. Drain, if necessary, and set aside.

❺ In the same saucepan, heat the remaining 2 tablespoons of oil over medium heat. Add the rice in small quantities and stir until well coated with oil. Add the vegetables and mix thoroughly.

● Makes 4 servings.

This "sun" rice dish is not only appealing but will certainly rank as a favorite.

Chicken with Two Types of Mushrooms

Preparation time: 13 min.
Cooking time: 18 min.

3 cups dried black mushrooms
1 tbsp. salted black beans (soybeans)
2 chicken breasts, skinned, boned and shredded
2 tbsp. mushroom soy sauce
1/3 cup (75 mL) sherry
2 tbsp. tapioca starch
3 tbsp. vegetable oil
2 cloves garlic, minced
2 - 10 oz. (284 mL) cans button mushrooms, drained
1 1/2 cups (375 mL) water
Salt

❶ Soak dried mushrooms in hot water for 1 to 2 hours, or until softened. Drain and cut off the stems.

❷ Rinse the salted black beans under cold water in a strainer. Set aside.

❸ Drizzle the shredded chicken with 1 tablespoon of mushroom soy sauce and 2 tablespoons of sherry. Dust with 1 tablespoon of tapioca starch; mix well.

❹ Heat oil in a wok over high heat and sauté garlic; add the black beans and the chicken; cook for about 5 minutes, stirring. Lower the heat and remove chicken from wok. Keep warm. Leave the black beans in the wok.

❺ Toss in the 2 different kinds of mushrooms and cook for a few minutes, stirring occasionally.

❻ Mix 1 tablespoon of tapioca starch with the remaining sherry, water and 1 tablespoon of mushroom soy sauce. Pour into the wok. Return the chicken to the wok and mix. Cook over low heat, stirring until sauce thickens. Add salt to taste.

❼ Serve with rice.

• Makes 4 servings.

REMARK: *Black mushrooms, black beans, mushroom soy sauce and tapioca starch are available year-round in Chinese foodstores. Salted black beans are fermented and should be washed before using.*

Chicken with Two Types of Mushrooms

Chicken with Creamy Spinach

Preparation time: 20 min.
Cooking time: 40 min.

10 oz. (284 g) fresh spinach
4 - 5 oz. (140 g) chicken breast halves, skinned and boned
2 cloves garlic, minced
3 tbsp. butter
2 tbsp. all-purpose flour
1/4 cup (60 mL) dry white wine
1 cup (250 mL) chicken broth
1/3 cup (75 mL) sour cream
1/3 cup (75 mL) milk
1 1/3 cups (135 g) grated mild cheddar cheese
2 tbsp. grated Parmesan cheese
White pepper
Salt

Chicken with Creamy Spinach *(cont'd)*

❶ Parboil the spinach for 2 minutes in boiling water; drain, then chop finely. Set aside.

❷ Pound chicken breasts with a meat mallet. Lightly sprinkle with pepper, salt and garlic. Heat 2 tablespoons of butter in a skillet over medium-high heat and sauté chicken until browned on both sides. Set aside.

❸ In a saucepan, melt the remaining 1 tablespoon of butter over medium heat and add the drained spinach. Cook for a few minutes, stirring. Sprinkle with flour and blend well. Pour in white wine and chicken broth. Blend well.

❹ Add sour cream, milk, 1/3 cup (30 g) of grated cheese and Parmesan cheese. Cook over low heat, stirring constantly, until sauce thickens.

❺ Pour the creamy spinach in an ovenproof shallow baking dish and place the chicken breasts on top. Sprinkle with remaining grated cheese and bake in a 350°F (175°C) oven for about 10 minutes, or until bubbly.

• Makes 4 servings.

Zucchini-Shrimp Quiche

Preparation time: 35 min.
Cooking time: 50 min.
Refrigeration time: 15 min.

PASTRY:

2 cups (275 g) all-purpose flour
Pinch of salt
1/3 cup (75 g) butter
1/4 cup (60 g) shortening
1/3 cup (75 mL) + 1 tbsp. cold water
1 egg, lightly beaten

❶ Sift flour and salt in a large mixing bowl and shape into a ring.

❷ Cut butter and shortening into pieces and place in the center of the ring. With a pastry blender or two knives, cut into the flour until mixture resembles small beans. Gradually sprinkle water over particles and mix until pastry is moistened. Gather into a ball and refrigerate 15 minutes.

❸ On a lightly floured surface, roll out dough to 1/4-inch (6-mm) thickness. Line a 9-inch (23-cm) pie plate without stretching dough.

❹ Brush pastry with egg and prick bottom with a fork.

❺ Bake in a preheated 400°F (200°C) oven for 15 minutes.

Zucchini-Shrimp Quiche (cont'd)

FILLING:

2 tbsp. butter
1 large zucchini, cut into ¼-inch (6-mm) slices
1 cup large fresh shrimp, shelled and deveined (leave tail shell attached)
1 tsp. minced green onion (scallion)
2 egg yolks
2 eggs
¼ cup (25 g) grated mild cheddar cheese
2 tbsp. all-purpose flour
¾ cup (170 mL) milk
Dash of white pepper
Dash of salt

❶ Heat butter in a skillet and sauté zucchini over medium-high heat until light golden brown. Remove from skillet and set aside.

❷ Add shrimp and green onion to skillet and sauté in leftover butter for a few minutes. Set aside.

❸ Combine egg yolks, eggs, grated cheese, flour, salt and pepper. Pour in milk and stir until well blended.

❹ Arrange the zucchini slices in bottom of baked pastry shell in an overlapping pattern. Fill the center with the shrimp, tails up. Pour in the milk mixture.

❺ Bake in a preheated 350°F (175°C) oven for 25 to 30 minutes or until a wooden skewer inserted in the center comes out clean.

● Makes 4 to 6 servings.

Veal Shanks with Grapes

Preparation time: 5 min.
Cooking time: 85 min.

4 - ¾ lb. (340 g) sliced veal shanks
1 cup (250 mL) sherry
2 tbsp. vegetable oil
1 cup (250 mL) white grape juice
1¼ cups (310 mL) water
2 tbsp. butter
1 cup seedless green grapes
1 cup seedless red grapes
1½ tbsp. tapioca starch
Black pepper
Salt
1 cup seedless green grapes (to garnish)

Veal Shanks with Grapes (cont'd)

❶ Drizzle the veal shanks with 2 tablespoons of sherry. Season with salt and pepper. Heat 1 tablespoon of oil over high heat in a pressure cooker and brown the sliced shanks on both sides, one by one. Add 1 tablespoon of oil, if necessary, between cooking. Set aside.

❷ Pour ¾ cup (170 mL) of sherry, ¾ cup (170 mL) of grape juice and ¼ cup (60 mL) of water into the pressure cooker; mix well. Put all the shanks in the pressure cooker and dot with butter. Cover and cook for 40 minutes over medium heat after pot whistles.

❸ Let the steam out and when there is no pressure, carefully open the cooker. Remove the shanks with a slotted spatula and keep warm.

❹ Toss in the green and red grapes and add remaining sherry and grape juice. Mix 1 cup (250 mL) of water with tapioca starch and stir into the mixture. Bring to a boil; reduce the heat and simmer for 25 to 30 minutes. Add salt to taste.

❺ Place veal shanks on a heated serving platter. Spoon sauce and cooked grapes over the shanks. Garnish with green grapes and serve immediately.

● Makes 4 servings.

Veal Roast with Pears

Preparation time: 20 min.
Cooking time: 90 min.

2 lb. (1 kg) veal roast
1 cup (250 mL) apple juice
2 tbsp. butter, softened
3 ripe pears, cored and thickly sliced
1/4 cup (60 mL) sherry
2 cups (500 mL) beef broth
Black pepper
Salt
1 pear, cored and sliced (to garnish)

❶ Place the roast on a rack in a greased shallow roasting pan.

❷ Slowly pour 1/2 cup (125 mL) of apple juice over the veal. Rub with pepper, salt and butter. Arrange the sliced pears around the veal and bake in a preheated 350°F (175°C) oven for 60 minutes.

❸ Every 15 minutes, drizzle the roast with 2 1/2 tablespoons of apple juice. Turn the roast after 30 minutes roasting. When ready, place the roast on a serving platter and keep warm.

❹ Scrape the bottom of the roast pan and gather all pan juices; pour into a small saucepan. Chill to solidify fat and remove, leaving only the caramelized drippings in the saucepan. Place on medium heat, then stir in sherry and beef broth. Add the cooked pears. Bring to a boil; let liquid bubble for 30 minutes to reduce, stirring frequently. Add salt to taste. Strain to collect liquid and pour over the roast.

❺ Garnish with a few pear slices and serve.

• Makes 4 servings.

Veal Roast with Pears

Veal Rolls with Black Beans —Chinese Style

Preparation time: 25 min.
Cooking time: 30 min.

10 oz. (280 g) rice vermicelli (2 packages)
⅓ cup (75 mL) vegetable oil
3 cloves garlic, minced
Light soy sauce
1 tsp. fish sauce
4 - 4 oz. (125 g) large veal scallops
Garlic powder
1 tbsp. fresh ginger, finely chopped
1 tbsp. salted black beans (soybeans)**
2 celery stalks, thinly and diagonally sliced
3 cups bean sprouts
1 tbsp. Chinese cooking wine
1 tbsp. tapioca starch
1 cup (250 mL) water
Salt

** Salted black beans (soy beans) are fermented and should be washed before using.

Veal Rolls with Black Beans
—Chinese Style (cont'd)

❶ Cook the vermicelli in slightly salted boiling water for 2 to 3 minutes. Drain. Rinse quickly through cold water and drain thoroughly. Set aside.

❷ In a large non-stick wok, heat 2 tablespoons of oil over medium heat and sauté 2 minced cloves of garlic. Add the vermicelli in small quantities and cook, stirring constantly, until coated with oil. The vermicelli must not stick together. Drizzle with 1 tablespoon of soy sauce and 1 teaspoon of fish sauce. Toss until well mixed. Remove from wok and keep warm.

❸ Pound veal scallops with a meat mallet. Lightly sprinkle with soy sauce and garlic powder. In a skillet, brown the scallops on both sides in 2 tablespoons of oil over high heat, one by one. Keep warm.

❹ Heat remaining oil over high heat in the wok and briefly sauté ginger, remaining minced garlic and black beans. Add the celery; stir-fry for 2 minutes, then add the bean sprouts and stir-fry for 2 minutes longer.

❺ Lower the heat. Stir in cooking wine and add salt to taste. Combine the tapioca starch with water, then pour over the vegetables; blend well. Cook until sauce thickens. Remove from heat.

❻ Spoon some vegetable mixture over the scallops and roll up loosely, securing with a wooden skewer.

❼ Arrange the scallops on a heated serving dish surrounded with vermicelli. Serve immediately.

• Makes 4 servings.

Marylin's Vermicelli

Preparation time: 12 min.
Cooking time: 30 min.

10 oz. (280 g) rice vermicelli
1 chicken breast, skinned, boned and shredded
1 - 1/2 lb. (225 g) turbot fillet, cut into bite-sized pieces
2 tbsp. light soy sauce
1/4 tsp. white pepper
2 cloves garlic, minced
1 tbsp. chopped fresh ginger
1/3 cup (75 mL) vegetable oil
3 carrots, grated
3 eggs
Salt

❶ Cook the vermicelli in lightly salted boiling water for 5 to 7 minutes until it becomes soft and loose. Drain. Rinse quickly under cold water and drain again. Set aside.

❷ Sprinkle chicken and fish with 2 teaspoons of soy sauce, pepper, garlic and ginger. Mix well.

❸ In a large non-stick wok, heat 3 tablespoons of oil over medium-high heat. Briefly stir-fry carrots.

❹ Add chicken and fish; cook for 3 to 4 minutes, stirring carefully, until fork-tender. Sprinkle with 1 teaspoon of soy sauce.

❺ Break in the eggs and mix vigorously until crumbly. Remove mixture from wok and keep warm.

❻ In the same wok, heat remaining oil over medium heat and add the vermicelli in small quantities. Cook for a few minutes, stirring, then drizzle with remaining soy sauce. Mix thoroughly until vermicelli is well coated with oil.

❼ Return the chicken-fish mixture to the wok. Lower the heat and mix together. Serve immediately.

● Makes 4 servings.

REMARK: *This tangy dish is perfect for party buffets, lunch or dinner. It can be prepared in advance and easily reheated in a microwave or a double boiler.*

Marylin's Vermicelli

Pork Roast with Honey and Cloves

Preparation time: 15 min.
Cooking time: 100 min.

2 lb. (1 kg) pork roast
1 1/3 cups (325 mL) cider
1 tsp. ground cinnamon
1/3 cup (75 mL) honey
1 tbsp. whole cloves
2 tsp. tapioca starch
1/4 cup (60 mL) apple juice
1 cup (250 mL) chicken broth
Dash salt
Dash black pepper
Apple slices (to garnish)

❶ Place the pork roast on a rack in a greased shallow roasting pan and drizzle with 1/4 cup (60 mL) of cider. Rub with cinnamon, salt and pepper. Brush with honey and stud with the cloves.

❷ Bake in a preheated 350°F (175°C) oven for 1 hour and 20 minutes.

❸ Every 20 minutes, drizzle the roast with 1/4 cup (60 mL) of cider and brush with some honey. Turn after 40 minutes roasting.

❹ When done, place the roast on a serving platter and keep warm.

❺ Pour the pan drippings into a saucepan. Chill and remove solidified fat on the surface. Place saucepan on medium heat. Stir in remaining cider. Combine tapioca starch, apple juice, chicken broth and a pinch of cinnamon and pour into the saucepan. Mix well and bring to a boil. Let liquid bubble for 20 minutes to reduce, stirring frequently.

❻ Add salt to taste and strain the sauce.

❼ Pour some of the sauce over the pork roast and garnish with apple slices. Serve the remaining sauce in a sauceboat.

• Makes 4 to 6 servings.

Pork Roast with Honey and Cloves

Asparagus-Chicken Soufflé

Preparation time: 30 min.
Cooking time: 45 min.

3 tbsp. butter
1/4 cup chopped onion
3 tbsp. all-purpose flour
1 1/4 cups (310 mL) milk
1 cup asparagus tips, cooked and finely chopped
2/3 cup (70 g) grated mild cheddar cheese
1 1/2 cups finely chopped cooked chicken breast
Dash of Tabasco
1/4 cup (60 mL) whipping cream
Pinch of white pepper
1/2 tsp. salt
4 eggs, separated
2 egg whites

❶ Melt butter in a skillet over medium heat and sauté onion. Stir in flour.

❷ Pour in milk and blend well. Cook over low heat until mixture thickens. Remove from heat. Add asparagus, cheese, chicken, Tabasco, cream, pepper and salt; mix thoroughly.

❸ Beat the egg yolks and fold into the mixture.

❹ With clean beaters, beat the egg whites until stiff and delicately fold into the mixture.

❺ Pour into a buttered 6-cup soufflé dish and bake in a preheated 375°F (190°C) oven for 35 minutes or until soufflé is golden brown and puffy.

❻ Serve immediately.

● Makes 4 servings.

Desserts

Peach Shortcake (page 122)

Banana Beignets des Alizés

Preparation time: 15 min.
Cooking time: 15 min.

3 ripe medium bananas, peeled
1 egg
1/4 cup (50 g) sugar
1/4 cup (60 mL) milk
1 1/2 tsp. vanilla extract
1 tbsp. dark rum
1/4 cup (30 g) all-purpose flour
Pinch of salt
1/2 cup (40 g) skimmed milk powder
1 tsp. sodium bicarbonate
1/2 cup (100 g) butter
Powdered sugar
1 cup (100 g) sweetened shredded coconut
1 carambola, sliced or 1 cup cherries (to garnish)

❶ Cut the three bananas in half. Press each half lightly and carefully with fingers in order to separate them into their 3 segments (see picture).

❷ In a medium mixing bowl, beat egg and sugar with an electric mixer until smooth; blend in milk, vanilla and rum.

❸ Sift together flour, salt, milk powder and sodium bicarbonate onto the egg mixture, beating until smooth.

❹ In a large non-stick skillet, melt 4 tablespoons of butter over medium heat. Dip each banana segment into the batter, coating well. Cook in butter until lightly browned, turning once.

❺ Cook only 4 to 6 segments at a time. Add more butter, if necessary.

❻ Drain on paper towels and let cool.

❼ To serve, sift powdered sugar generously over the beignets and sprinkle with shredded coconut. Garnish with a carambola star or a few cherries.

● Makes 4 to 6 servings.

Banana Beignets des Alizés

Banana-Coconut Ring Cake

Preparation time: 35 min.
Cooking time: 45 min.

½ cup (120 g) butter, softened
½ cup (120 g) cream cheese, softened
1 cup (180 g) granulated sugar
5 eggs, separated
1¼ cups (310 mL) puréed bananas
2 tsp. almond extract
½ cup (125 mL) coconut cream
½ cup (60 g) unsweetened shredded coconut
2 tbsp. dark rum (optional)
2½ cups (340 g) all-purpose flour
⅓ cup (30 g) cornstarch
1¼ tsp. baking powder
1¼ tsp. sodium bicarbonate
¼ tsp. salt
Powdered sugar (optional)

Banana-Coconut Ring Cake (cont'd)

❶ In a large bowl, beat together the butter, cream cheese and sugar until light and smooth.

❷ Add the egg yolks, one at a time, beating well after each addition.

❸ Beat in puréed bananas, almond extract, coconut cream, shredded coconut and the rum.

❹ Sift together flour, cornstarch, baking powder, sodium bicarbonate and salt onto the banana mixture, beating until well blended.

❺ With clean beaters, beat the egg whites until stiff. Gently fold into the batter.

❻ Turn into a greased fluted ring pan and bake in a preheated 350°F (175°C) oven for 45 minutes. Turn off the heat and leave the cake in the oven for 15 minutes longer.

❼ Remove cake from pan and let cool on a wire rack. Dust with powdered sugar, if desired.

● Makes 12 servings.

Vanilla Ice Cream

Preparation time: 10 min.
Cooking time: 5 min.
Freezing time: 20 min.+

1 envelope (1 tbsp. or 7 g) unflavored gelatin
1 cup (250 mL) milk
2 cups (500 mL) whipping cream
1 cup (180 g) sugar
1 1/2 tbsp. vanilla extract

❶ In a skillet, sprinkle the gelatin over milk and let stand for 5 minutes to soften. Cook over low heat, stirring until gelatin dissolves. Pour into a large mixing bowl. Cool.

❷ Whip the cream with sugar and vanilla until soft peaks form, then fold into the cooled milk mixture.

❸ Pour into an ice-cream maker and freeze according to the manufacturer's instructions (20 minutes). If you do not have an ice-cream maker, refer to the directions given for the recipe "Orange Ice Cream", page 109 for regular freezing procedures.

● Makes 4 to 6 servings.

Stuffed Lychees with Orange Cream and Watermelon Sauce

Preparation time: 35 min.
Cooking time: 8 min.
Chilling time: 30 min.

Stuffed Lychees with Orange Cream and Watermelon Sauce (cont'd)

1 or 2 slices watermelon, seeded
3 - 20 oz. (565 g) cans lychees, drained (reserve ²/₃ cup [150 mL] of the syrup to prepare the sauce)
½ cup (125 mL) orange juice
1 tsp. apricot liqueur
½ envelope (1½ tsp.) unflavored gelatin
1 tbsp. sugar
¼ cup (60 mL) whipping cream
¼ cup (60 mL) plain yogurt

❶ Cut regular small triangles with the watermelon slices and set aside.

❷ With a very sharp knife, lightly slit the bottom side (the pointed part) of the lychee for garnishing with watermelon triangles. Refrigerate.

❸ In a small non-stick skillet, combine orange juice and apricot liqueur. Sprinkle with gelatin and let stand for 5 minutes to soften. Cook over low heat, stirring until gelatin dissolves. Add sugar and stir until dissolved. Cool.

❹ Whip the cream until soft peaks form and fold into the orange juice-gelatin mixture.

❺ Blend in yogurt and chill for 8 minutes or until partially set. Beat again with the electric mixer.

❻ Stuff each lychee with orange cream, using a tiny spoon. Place them on a plate with their pointed sides up so that they do not roll around on the dish. Chill for half an hour or until cream is firm. Insert a melon triangle on top of each lychee.

❼ To serve, arrange the stuffed lychees on individual dessert dishes and spoon watermelon sauce (see recipe below) over lychees.

● Makes 6 servings.

WATERMELON SAUCE:

²/₃ cup (150 mL) lychee syrup (from can)
²/₃ cup (150 mL) puréed watermelon
1 tbsp. sugar
½ tsp. lemon juice
1 tbsp. cornstarch
¼ cup (60 mL) orange juice

❶ Pour the lychee syrup in a small non-stick saucepan. Stir in puréed watermelon, sugar and lemon juice.

❷ Combine cornstarch with orange juice and pour into saucepan. Cook over low heat, stirring until mixture thickens.

❸ Cool.

Guava Ice Cream

Preparation time: 15 min.
Cooking time: 7 min.
Freezing time: 20 min.+

1 cup (250 mL) milk
3 egg yolks
1/2 cup (100 g) sugar
1/3 cup (50 g) all-purpose flour
4 guavas, peeled
1 cup (250 mL) orange juice
1 1/3 cups (240 g) sugar
2 tbsp. lemon juice
2 cups (500 mL) whipping cream

❶ In a small saucepan, scald the milk.

❷ In a medium heatproof mixing bowl, beat egg yolks with sugar using an electric mixer until smooth. Stir in flour. Gradually pour in the scalded milk, stirring until well blended. Place bowl over simmering water and cook, stirring constantly, until mixture thickens. Cool this custard.

❸ Using a very sharp knife, remove the guava pulp carefully without taking any seeds.

❹ Place the orange juice, sugar, lemon juice and guava pulp in a blender and process until smoothly puréed. Pour into a large mixing bowl, then fold in the cooled custard.

❺ Whip the cream until soft peaks form and fold into the guava cream.

❻ Pour into an ice-cream maker container and freeze according to the manufacturer's instructions (20 minutes). If you do not have an ice-cream maker, follow the directions given for the recipe "Orange Ice Cream", page 109 for regular freezing procedures.

❼ Store the frozen ice cream in an airtight container.

● Makes 7 cups (1 3/4 litres).

Cheese-Chestnut Tart

Preparation time: 40 min.
Cooking time: 30 min.

CRUST:

1/4 cup (60 mL) melted butter
3 tbsp. sugar
1 cup (120 g) crushed graham crackers
1 tsp. lemon rind
1/4 tsp. vanilla extract

FILLING:
8 oz. (250 g) cream cheese, softened
1/4 cup (50 g) sugar
1 tbsp. lemon juice
1 tsp. vanilla extract
1 tsp. lemon rind
2 eggs
2 tbsp. all-purpose flour

CHESTNUT CREAM:

2/3 cup (150 mL) canned chestnut purée
3 tbsp. sweetened condensed milk
1 tsp. vanilla

To prepare the crust:

❶ Combine melted butter with sugar. Blend in remaining ingredients. Press firmly onto the bottom and sides of a 9 1/2-inch (24-cm) removable-bottom pie tin. Chill until ready to use.

To prepare the filling:

❷ Beat cream cheese and sugar with an electric mixer until light and smooth.

❸ Blend in lemon juice, vanilla, lemon rind and eggs (one at a time). Stir in flour and continue beating until thoroughly mixed.

❹ Turn into the chilled crust.

To prepare the cream:

❺ In a small mixing bowl, beat together chestnut purée with condensed milk and vanilla until smooth. Pour into the crust over the cream cheese mixture. With a small spatula, carefully mix the chestnut cream with the cheese in a circular motion. This will create a light marble look.

❻ Bake in a preheated 350°F (175°C) oven for 20 to 25 minutes or until a wooden pick inserted in the center comes out clean.

❼ Allow to cool.

Cheese-Chestnut Tart (cont'd)

DECORATION:

¾ cup (170 mL) chestnut purée
2 tbsp. sweetened condensed milk
1 tbsp. powdered sugar
1 tsp. vanilla extract
¼ cup (30 g) ground nuts
Whole nuts

To decorate:

❽ Beat together chestnut purée, condensed milk, sugar and vanilla until smooth. Spoon mixture into a pastry bag fitted with a ¼-inch (6-mm) star tube and pipe rosettes around the edge and in the center of the tart. Sprinkle with ground nuts and garnish with whole nuts.

● Makes 8 servings.

An eye-appealing tart that will impress all your guests.

Riche-Terre Pineapple Crêpes

Preparation time: 50 min.
Cooking time: 35 min.
Chilling time: 60 min.

BATTER:
3 eggs
Pinch of salt
2 tbsp. sugar
¼ tsp. lemon juice
1 tbsp. dark rum
1¼ cups (310 mL) milk
1 cup (140 g) all-purpose flour
¼ cup (60 mL) melted butter

❶ In a small mixing bowl, combine eggs, salt, sugar, lemon juice and rum and beat with an electric mixer at low speed until smooth.

❷ Alternately beat in milk and flour in small quantities. Blend in melted butter. Refrigerate batter for one hour.

❸ Place a non-stick skillet over medium heat and brush with butter. Pour in ¼ cup (60 mL) of batter. Lift and tilt the skillet in a circular motion in order to spread batter over the bottom of the skillet. Cook until light golden brown; carefully turn the crêpe with a plastic spatula and cook the other side. There is no need to grease the skillet for cooking remaining batter.

❹ Separate each crêpe with waxed paper and set aside.

● Makes 14 crêpes.

REMARK: To store cooked crêpes, separate them with waxed paper before wrapping in plastic bag or enclosing in an airtight container.

Riche-Terre Pineapple Crêpes (cont'd)

FILLING:

2 egg yolks
1 egg
½ cup (105 g) sugar
1¼ tsp. vanilla extract
3 tbsp. cornstarch
1¾ cups (420 mL) milk
1 - 19 oz. (540 mL) can pineapple chunks, drained (reserve the syrup) or 1 fresh pineapple, pared and cut into small pieces + ⅓ cup (75 mL) pineapple juice
⅓ cup (40 g) sweetened shredded coconut
⅓ cup (75 mL) whipping cream
1 - 8 oz. (227 mL) can pineapple rings, drained (to garnish)

❶ In a heat-resistant bowl, combine egg yolks and egg, sugar, vanilla and cornstarch, and beat with an electric mixer until smooth.

❷ Scald milk in a saucepan. Gradually pour over the cornstarch mixture, blending well. Return to saucepan and cook over low heat, stirring until thickened. Cool. Stir this custard frequently to prevent formation of a skin on the surface.

❸ In an electric blender, process until smooth 1 cup of drained pineapple chunks with ⅓ cup (75 mL) of the syrup or ⅓ cup (75 mL) pineapple juice (if you use fresh pineapple). Stir into the cooled custard.

❹ Divide pineapple cream and remaining pineapple pieces between crêpes. Fold over.

❺ Serve crêpes chilled, sprinkled with shredded coconut and topped with rosettes of whipped cream. Garnish with a pineapple ring.

● Makes 14 servings.

REMARK: *Crêpes can be filled and garnished a few hours before serving. Refrigerate.*

Creamy Pineapple Cheesecake

Preparation time: 65 min.
Chilling time: 4 hrs.
(incl. cooling period)

CRUST:

1¼ cups (150 g) crushed coconut cookies
1 cup (120 g) crushed graham crackers
1 tsp. cinnamon
¼ tsp. nutmeg
⅓ cup (75 mL) melted butter

FILLING:

2 envelopes (2 tbsp. or 14 g) unflavored gelatin
⅔ cup (150 mL) pineapple juice
3 eggs, separated
8 oz. (250 g) cream cheese, softened
1 cup (180 g) sugar
1 cup (250 mL) sour cream
1 tbsp. lemon rind
2½ tbsp. lemon juice or juice of 1 lemon
½ tsp. vanilla extract
½ cup (125 mL) whipping cream
5 pineapple rings (canned), drained
Cinnamon (to garnish)
⅓ cup (75 mL) whipping cream (to garnish)

To prepare the crust:

❶ Mix together the crushed coconut cookies, crushed graham crackers, cinnamon, nutmeg and butter. Press firmly onto bottom and sides of an 8½-inch (22-cm) springform pan. Chill until ready to use.

To prepare the filling:

❷ In a non-stick skillet, soak the gelatin in pineapple juice for 5 minutes to soften. Cook over low heat, stirring until gelatin is dissolved. Remove from heat.

❸ Beat egg yolks until creamy. Stir into the gelatin mixture. Cool.

❹ Beat the cream cheese with sugar until light and smooth. Blend in the sour cream, lemon rind, lemon juice and vanilla. Stir in the gelatin mixture.

❺ Whip cream until soft peaks form and fold into the cheese mixture.

❻ Beat the egg whites using clean beaters until stiff and gently fold into the cheese mixture.

❼ Pour half of the cheese preparation into the chilled crust and arrange 4 pineapple rings on the surface. Pour the remaining cheese mixture over the pineapple rings. Chill for about 4 hours or until firm.

❽ Dust with cinnamon and garnish with 1 pineapple ring and rosettes of whipped cream.

● Makes 8 servings.

Creamy Pineapple Cheesecake

Tropical-Sun Cake

Preparation time: 20 min.
Freezing time: 3 to 4 hrs.

1 cup pineapple chunks, fresh or canned, drained
½ cup (125 mL) pineapple juice
2 cups (500 mL) plain yogurt
¾ cup (150 g) sugar**
½ cup (60 g) ground vanilla biscuits
½ cup (60 g) ground almonds
¼ cup (60 mL) coconut milk
½ cup (125 mL) whipping cream
¼ large watermelon
3 tbsp. powdered sugar
1 carambola, thinly sliced (optional)
1 cup watermelon balls or pomegranate seeds

** Increase the sugar to 1 cup if you use fresh pineapple.

Tropical-Sun Cake (cont'd)

❶ Process pineapple chunks with pineapple juice and yogurt in an electric blender until smooth. Pour into a large mixing bowl.

❷ With an electric mixer, blend in sugar, ground biscuits, ground almonds and coconut milk.

❸ Whip cream until soft peaks form and fold into pineapple mixture.

❹ Turn into an oiled 6-cup mold or into individual molds and freeze until firm.

❺ Meanwhile, prepare the watermelon sauce. Remove seeds from watermelon and process, with powdered sugar, in an electric blender until smooth. Chill.

❻ To serve, gently unmold the pineapple ice-cream cake onto a dessert dish. Pour watermelon sauce over and garnish with carambola stars, watermelon balls or pomegranate seeds.

• Makes 6 to 8 servings.

Orange Ice Cream

Preparation time: 25 min.
Cooking time: 20 min.
Freezing time: 20 min.+

1½ cups (375 mL) milk
⅓ cup (50 g) all-purpose flour
1 cup (180 g) sugar
3 egg yolks, beaten
1 cup (250 mL) frozen orange juice concentrate, thawed
1 tsp. lemon juice
1 tbsp. orange rind
2 cups (500 mL) whipping cream

❶ In a small saucepan, scald 1 cup (250 mL) of milk.

❷ In another saucepan, combine remaining milk with flour and mix until smooth. Gradually add the scalded milk while stirring. Blend in sugar, then the egg yolks. Cook over low heat, stirring constantly, until thickened. Cool. Turn into a large mixing bowl.

❸ With an electric mixer, beat in orange juice concentrate, lemon juice, and rind.

❹ Whip cream until soft peaks form, then fold into the mixture.

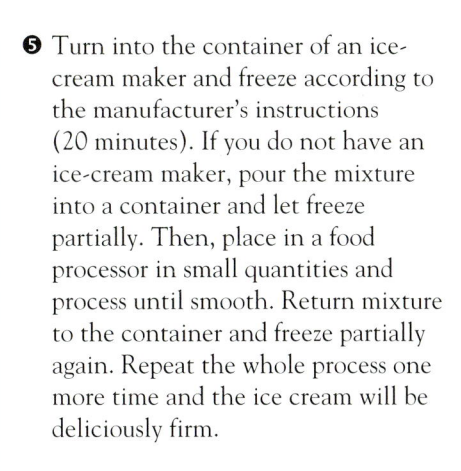

❺ Turn into the container of an ice-cream maker and freeze according to the manufacturer's instructions (20 minutes). If you do not have an ice-cream maker, pour the mixture into a container and let freeze partially. Then, place in a food processor in small quantities and process until smooth. Return mixture to the container and freeze partially again. Repeat the whole process one more time and the ice cream will be deliciously firm.

• Makes 8 cups (2 litres) of ice cream.

Grenadine Watermelon Mousse

Preparation time: 25 min.
Cooking time: 8 min.
Chilling time: 4 hrs.

2½ cups (625 mL) puréed watermelon
½ cup (125 mL) grenadine
3 eggs, separated
⅔ cup (120 g) sugar
1½ envelopes (1½ tbsp. or 10 g) unflavored gelatin
2 tbsp. lemon juice
1 tbsp. lime juice
¾ cup (170 mL) whipping cream
Watermelon balls (to garnish)
Mint leaves (to garnish)

❶ In a small non-stick saucepan, pour 1 cup (250 mL) of puréed watermelon and grenadine. Heat through.

❷ In a bowl, beat the egg yolks with sugar until creamy. Gradually stir in the hot watermelon-grenadine mixture. Place the bowl over a saucepan containing simmering water and cook for a few minutes, stirring constantly until mixture becomes thicker and smooth. Remove from heat.

❸ In a small non-stick saucepan, sprinkle gelatin over ½ cup (125 mL) of puréed watermelon and let stand for 5 minutes to soften. Cook over low heat, stirring until gelatin is dissolved. Stir into mixture. Cool.

❹ Pour mixture into a large bowl and add remaining puréed watermelon, lemon juice and lime juice. Mix thoroughly. Chill for 5 minutes.

❺ Meanwhile, whip cream until soft peaks form and beat egg whites with clean beaters until stiff. Gently fold both (whipped cream first) into watermelon mixture.

❻ Turn into an oiled 6-cup mold or into individual serving molds. Chill until firm (for about 4 hours).

❼ To serve, carefully unmold onto serving dish and garnish with watermelon balls and mint leaves.

● Makes 6 to 8 servings.

Grenadine Watermelon Mousse

Corn Pudding with Coconut

Preparation time: 5 min.
Cooking time: 12 min.

3 cups (750 mL) milk
1 cup (160 g) cornmeal (medium grind)
1/2 cup (70 g) brown sugar
1/3 cup (40 g) raisins
1/2 tsp. vanilla extract
1/2 tsp. cardamom powder
2 tbsp. butter
1/2 cup (60 g) sweetened shredded coconut
Candied cherries (to garnish)

Corn Pudding with Coconut (cont'd)

❶ Scald milk in a non-stick skillet over medium heat, then stir in cornmeal.

❷ Add sugar, raisins, vanilla, cardamom and butter. Stir and bring to a boil. Reduce the heat and cook, stirring constantly, until cornmeal softens, mixture thickens, and all the milk is absorbed. Remove from heat. Cool to lukewarm.

❸ Grease a 6-cup mold with butter and spread ¼ cup (30 g) of shredded coconut over the bottom. Turn pudding into mold and refrigerate overnight to firm.

❹ When ready to serve, carefully unmold the pudding onto a dessert dish and top with the remaining shredded coconut. Garnish with candied cherries.

• Makes 4 to 6 servings.

Shortcake with Chestnut Cream

Preparation time: 70 min.
Cooking time: 25 min.

SHORT PASTRY:

2 cups (275 g) all-purpose flour
1 cup (225 g) butter, cut into small pieces
1 tbsp. sugar
⅓ cup (75 mL) apple jelly

❶ Shape a ring with the flour and place butter and sugar in the center. With a pastry blender or two knives, cut in butter until mixture becomes crumbly. Mix until dough becomes smooth, then gather into a ball. Refrigerate for 15 minutes.

❷ Roll out dough to ¼-inch (6-mm) thickness on a lightly floured surface and cut out circles with a 2-inch (5-cm) diameter fluted cutter.

❸ Place on a greased cookie sheet and bake in a preheated 350°F (175°C) oven for 15 to 20 minutes or until light golden brown.

❹ Let cool. Meanwhile, melt the apple jelly and apply a thick coating on each round of pastry. Set aside.

● Makes 28 shortcakes.

Shortcake with Chestnut Cream (cont'd)

CHESTNUT CREAM:

½ cup (125 mL) milk
1 envelope (1 tbsp. or 7 g) unflavored gelatin
1½ cups (375 mL) chestnut purée
1 cup (100 g) powdered sugar
2 tbsp. vanilla extract
1 tsp. instant coffee
2 tbsp. Tia Maria liqueur
½ cup (125 mL) whipping cream
Sliced almonds, toasted (to garnish)

❶ Pour milk in a small saucepan and sprinkle gelatin over milk. Let stand for 5 minutes to soften, then dissolve over low heat, stirring. Cool to lukewarm.

❷ Combine chestnut purée, powdered sugar, vanilla, coffee and liqueur in a medium-sized bowl and beat at high speed with an electric mixer until smooth and creamy.

❸ Blend in the milk-gelatin mixture.

❹ Whip the cream until stiff peaks form, then fold into the chestnut cream.

❺ Chill for 15 minutes or until partially set, then beat again. Put back in the refrigerator and chill for 10 to 15 minutes longer or until mixture is thick enough to be piped.

❻ Spoon cream into a pastry bag affixed with a ½-inch (12-mm) star tube, then pipe rosettes over the shortcake circles.

❼ Garnish with toasted sliced almonds.

REMARK: *The shortcakes can be prepared ahead of time. A few hours before serving, prepare the chestnut cream and pipe rosettes over the shortcakes. Garnish with toasted sliced almonds.*

Mango Parfait

Preparation time: 15 min.

1 recipe Vanilla Ice Cream, page 99
$^1/_2$ cup (40 g) toasted sliced almonds
1 cup (120 g) ground almonds
1 cup (250 mL) whipped cream
1 firm ripe mango, peeled and diced

❶ Place a scoop of ice cream in a parfait glass. Sprinkle generously with toasted sliced almonds and ground almonds. Pour 2 tablespoons of mango sauce (see recipe below) over ice cream.

❷ Repeat the whole process once or twice to fill up the glass.

❸ Garnish with dollops of whipped cream and some diced mango pulp.

● Makes 4 servings.

MANGO SAUCE:

1 ripe mango, peeled and cut into small pieces
1 cup (250 mL) pineapple juice
$^1/_3$ cup (60 g) sugar
1 tbsp. apricot liqueur (optional)

❶ Place the mango together with the pineapple juice, sugar and apricot liqueur (optional) in a blender and process until smooth.

❷ Chill.

Pear Flan

Preparation time: 45 min.
Cooking time: 15 min.
(including cooling period)

CRUST:

¼ cup (60 mL) melted butter
¼ cup (50 g) sugar
¼ tsp. vanilla extract
Pinch of salt
1 cup (120 g) crushed graham crackers

FILLING:

2 cups (500 mL) milk
⅓ cup (75 mL) pear syrup (from can)
3 egg yolks
½ cup (100 g) sugar
1 tsp. vanilla extract
⅓ cup (30 g) cornstarch
1 envelope (1 tbsp. or 7 g) unflavored gelatin
1 small can pears, drained and sliced to ¼-inch (6-mm) thickness (reserve the syrup)
½ cup (125 mL) whipping cream (decoration)

❶ Mix together butter and sugar. Add remaining ingredients, blending well. Press onto bottom and sides of a removable-bottom 9-inch (23-cm) pie tin. Chill.

❷ In a saucepan, scald 1½ cups (375 mL) of milk. Combine pear syrup, egg yolks, sugar, vanilla and cornstarch in a bowl. Mix until smooth. Gradually stir in the scalded milk and return to saucepan. Cook over low heat, stirring constantly, until mixture thickens. Cool this custard to lukewarm.

❸ In a small saucepan, soak gelatin in remaining milk for 5 minutes to soften. Cook over low heat, stirring until gelatin dissolves. Blend into the warm custard and let cool, stirring from time to time to prevent film formation.

❹ Meanwhile, arrange a pattern of pear slices at the bottom of the chilled crust and pour in the cooled custard, evenly smoothing the surface.

❺ Chill until set (2 to 3 hours).

❻ Decorate with rosettes of whipped cream and pieces of pear.

● Makes 8 servings.

Pear Flan

Island Fruit Salad

Preparation time: 18 min.

1 carambola, thinly sliced into stars
1 firm ripe papaya, peeled and seeded
1 medium banana, peeled
¼ watermelon
1 grapefruit
Juice of 1 lemon or 2 tbsp.
3 tbsp. powdered sugar
¼ cup (60 mL) kirsch (optional)

REMARK: When buying carambolas, pick the ones that are firm, bright yellow and glossy looking with a velvety and "wax" texture.

Island Fruit Salad (cont'd)

❶ Dice the papaya or scoop out balls with a Parisian cutter.

❷ Slice the banana thinly and diagonally.

❸ Scoop out watermelon balls.

❹ Peel the grapefruit and remove skinless segments with a very sharp knife.

❺ Put all the pieces of fruit in a salad bowl; drizzle lemon juice over all pieces and toss gently to mix.

❻ Dust with powdered sugar and drizzle with kirsch.

❼ Mix thoroughly and serve chilled.

● Makes 4 to 6 servings.

Orange-Chocolate Mousse Cake

Preparation time: 65 min.
(including cooling period)
Cooking time: 25 min.
Chilling time: 4 hrs.

This elegant dessert can be prepared in advance and will keep well in the refrigerator for a few days. It will always deserve a place in any festive celebration.

Orange-Chocolate Mousse Cake (cont'd)

CAKE:

1 egg, separated
2 tbsp. sugar
2 tbsp. all-purpose flour
Pinch of salt
1 tsp. baking powder
1 egg white
2 tbsp. Cointreau

❶ Beat the egg yolk with sugar until creamy.

❷ Sift the flour, salt and baking powder onto egg mixture. Beat until thoroughly blended.

❸ Wash the beaters thoroughly, then beat the egg whites until stiff. Fold gently into flour mixture.

❹ Turn into a greased loaf pan and bake in a preheated 350°F (175°C) oven for about 7 minutes or until cake is light golden brown and sides are slightly detached from pan.

❺ Cool on a wire rack. Line the mold with clear plastic wrap or foil, leaving the sides overlapping to facilitate handling when mousse is set. Put the cake back in the mold and drizzle with Cointreau. Chill until ready to use.

ORANGE MOUSSE:

1 1/4 cups (310 mL) orange juice
1 envelope (1 tbsp. or 7 g) unflavored gelatin
1/3 cup (60 g) sugar
1 egg yolk, beaten
1/3 cup (75 mL) whipping cream
2 egg whites
1/4 tsp. tartar cream

❶ In a non-stick skillet, sprinkle the gelatin over orange juice and let stand for 5 minutes to soften. Cook over low heat, stirring until gelatin dissolves.

❷ Add sugar and beaten egg yolk. Cook over low heat, stirring constantly until mixture thickens. Cool.

❸ Whip cream until soft peaks form, then fold into the orange-juice mixture.

❹ With clean beaters, beat the egg whites with tartar cream until stiff. Fold gently into the mixture.

❺ Chill mixture for 8 to 10 minutes or until slightly thickened. Beat again with the electric mixer and pour into the lined loaf pan over the cake, evenly smoothing the surface. Refrigerate while the chocolate mousse is being prepared.

Orange-Chocolate Mousse Cake *(cont'd)*

CHOCOLATE MOUSSE:

1 cup (250 mL) milk
1 envelope (1 tbsp. or 7 g) unflavored gelatin
1/3 cup (60 g) sugar
1/2 oz. (14 g) unsweetened chocolate
1 tsp. instant coffee
1 tbsp. Tia Maria liqueur
1/2 cup (125 mL) whipping cream
2 egg whites
1/4 tsp. tartar cream
Orange segments
1/2 cup (125 mL) whipping cream (to garnish)

❶ Pour the milk in a small saucepan or skillet and sprinkle gelatin over the milk. Let stand for 5 minutes to soften and cook over low heat, stirring until gelatin dissolves.

❷ Add sugar and blend well to dissolve. Remove from heat.

❸ Melt the chocolate over simmering water and alternately add coffee and milk mixture in small quantities, blending well. Stir in Tia Maria. Cool.

❹ Whip the cream until soft peaks form and gently fold into the chocolate-milk mixture.

❺ Beat the egg whites with tartar cream (using clean beaters) until stiff and gently fold into the mixture.

❻ Pour over the firm orange mousse, evenly smoothing the surface. Chill for 2 to 3 hours or until set.

❼ To serve, slowly pull the mousse cake out of the loaf pan and carefully peel off the plastic wrap or foil. Cut into 8 equal slices. Pour 1/4 cup (60 mL) of orange sauce (see recipe below) in a dessert dish and place a slice of orange-chocolate mousse cake in the center.

❽ Garnish with orange segments and rosettes of whipped cream.

• Makes 8 servings.

Orange Sauce

Preparation time: 5 min.
Cooking time: 5 min.

ORANGE SAUCE:

1 1/4 cups (310 mL) orange juice
1 1/2 tbsp. cornstarch
1 tbsp. Cointreau
1/3 cup (60 g) sugar

❶ Combine juice and cornstarch; mix thoroughly. Pour into a small non-stick saucepan. Stir in Cointreau and sugar. Cook over low heat, stirring constantly until mixture becomes thick and smooth. Remove from heat; cool and chill until ready to serve.

• Makes 8 servings.

Peach Shortcake

Preparation time: 45 min.
Cooking time: 25 min.

1 - 14 oz. (398 mL) can sliced peaches, drained
1²/₃ cups (230 g) all-purpose flour
2 tbsp. sugar
2 tsp. baking powder
¼ tsp. salt
½ cup (120 g) butter
¼ cup (60 mL) whipping cream
⅓ cup (75 mL) milk

❶ Thinly slice the peaches.

❷ Combine flour, sugar, baking powder and salt in a large mixing bowl. Shape into a ring and place butter in the center. Cut in with two knives or a pastry blender until mixture becomes crumbly.

❸ Gradually add cream and milk and knead until dough becomes smooth. Gather into a ball.

❹ Roll out pastry to ½-inch (12-mm) thickness on a lightly floured surface and cut out circles with a doughnut cutter. Place on a greased cookie sheet and bake in a preheated 400°F (200°C) oven for 12 to 15 minutes or until light golden brown. Let cool on sheet.

❺ Cut each pastry circle in half, horizontally. Coat the bottom parts thickly with custard (see recipe next page) and arrange a few thin peach slices over the custard, leaving the outer edges free for piping in Chantilly cream (see recipe next page).

❻ Fill an icing bag, fitted with a ¼-inch (6-mm) star tube, with Chantilly cream and pipe rosettes around the outer edges of the pastries. Top with the remaining halved pastries.

Peach Shortcake *(cont'd)*

❼ Dice some of the sliced peaches and fill up the holes in the center. Pour some of the remaining custard over the diced peaches into the holes and dust the entire surface with powdered sugar. Pipe Chantilly cream around the outer edges of shortcakes and garnish with diced peaches.

❽ Chill.

• Makes 6 shortcakes.

CUSTARD:

1¼ cups (310 mL) milk
¼ cup (30 g) cornstarch
2 egg yolks, beaten
2 tbsp. sugar
¼ tsp. vanilla

❶ Scald 1 cup (250 mL) of milk in a small saucepan.

❷ Meanwhile, combine cornstarch with remaining milk in a heat-resistant bowl. Stir in beaten egg yolks, sugar and vanilla.

❸ Gradually pour scalded milk over the cornstarch mixture, blending well. Return to saucepan and cook over low heat, stirring until mixture thickens.

❹ Allow to cool and in the meantime, prepare the Chantilly cream.

CHANTILLY CREAM:

1 cup (250 mL) whipping cream
2 tbsp. powdered sugar
1 tbsp. peach liqueur
1 egg white

❶ Whip the cream together with sugar and liqueur until stiff peaks form.

❷ Using clean beaters, beat the egg white until stiff and gently fold into the whipped cream.

See photograph on page 95.

Pineapple Sherbet

Preparation time: 10 min.
Cooking time: 15 min.
Freezing time: 20 min.+

1¼ cups (225 g) sugar
1 cup (250 mL) water
1 - 19 oz. (540 mL) can pineapple chunks, undrained
1 tbsp. lemon juice
1 egg white

❶ Combine sugar and water in a medium saucepan and stir over low heat until sugar is dissolved. Bring to a boil. Lower the heat and simmer for 10 to 15 minutes to thicken. Cool.

❷ Place the undrained pineapple chunks in a blender. Process until smooth. Add the cooled syrup and lemon juice. Blend thoroughly.

❸ Pour the mixture into a large bowl. Beat the egg white until stiff and fold into the pineapple mixture.

❹ Place in an ice-cream maker container and freeze according to the manufacturer's instructions (20 minutes). If you do not have an ice-cream maker, follow the directions given for the recipe "Orange Ice Cream", page 109 for regular freezing procedures.

• Makes 4 cups (1 litre).

Guava Soufflé

Preparation time: 25 min.
Cooking time: 4 min.
Freezing time: 2 to 3 hrs.

2 large guavas, peeled
1/2 cup (125 mL) plain yogurt
1/2 cup (125 mL) apple juice
1 1/2 tsp. lime juice
1 cup (250 mL) milk
1 envelope (1 tbsp. or 7 g) unflavored gelatin
3 egg yolks
2/3 cup (120 g) sugar
2/3 cup (150 mL) whipping cream
6 egg whites
1 tsp. cream of tartar
1 cup (120 g) shredded coconut, unsweetened
Halved candied cherries (to garnish)

The subtle fragrance of the guava is heavenly! This dessert will undoubtedly be long-remembered by your guests.

Guava Soufflé (cont'd)

❶ Extend the collar of 6 small soufflé dishes 3 inches by securely taping waxed paper or foil around the dishes from the outside.

❷ With a very sharp knife, carefully remove the guava pulp without taking in any seeds. Place the pulp in an electric blender together with yogurt, apple and lime juices and process at high speed until smooth.

❸ In a small saucepan, soak the gelatin in milk for 5 minutes to soften. Cook over low heat, stirring until gelatin is dissolved. Cool to lukewarm, then add to the guava purée in the blender. Mix thoroughly.

❹ Beat the egg yolks with sugar until creamy. Add to the guava mixture in the blender and mix thoroughly. Pour into a large mixing bowl and chill for 5 minutes or until mixture mounds slightly when dropped from a spoon.

❺ Whip the cream until soft peaks form, then fold into the guava mixture.

❻ Wash the beaters thoroughly. Beat the egg whites with tartar cream until stiff and gently fold into the guava mixture.

❼ Turn into the prepared small soufflé dishes and freeze for about 2 hours or until firm, then refrigerate.

❽ To serve, remove collar around the dishes and sprinkle shredded coconut atop. Garnish with halved candied cherries.

● Makes 6 servings.

Heavenly Lychee Soufflé

Preparation time: 30 min.
Cooking time: 4 min.
Chilling time: 3 to 4 hrs.

1 - 20 oz. (565 g) can lychees, drained (reserve 1 cup [250 mL] of the syrup)
1½ envelopes (1½ tbsp. or 10 g) unflavored gelatin
1 cup (250 mL) milk
2 tbsp. lemon juice
½ cup (100 g) sugar
1 tbsp. lime juice
¼ cup (60 mL) coconut milk
½ cup (125 mL) whipping cream
4 egg whites
1 tsp. tartar cream
Pomegranate seeds (to garnish)

❶ Extend the collar of 6 small soufflé dishes 3 inches by securely taping waxed paper or foil around the dishes from the outside.

❷ In a small non-stick skillet, sprinkle gelatin over the lychee syrup. Let stand for 5 minutes to soften. Cook over low heat, stirring until gelatin dissolves. Cool to lukewarm.

❸ Put the lychees, milk, lemon juice, sugar, lime juice and coconut milk in an electric blender and process at high speed until smooth. Blend in the gelatin mixture and pour into a large mixing bowl.

❹ Whip the cream until soft peaks form and fold into the lychee mixture. Chill for 5 minutes.

❺ Wash the beaters thoroughly. Beat the egg whites with tartar cream until stiff and gently fold into the mixture. Chill for 5 minutes longer or until mixture is slightly thickened, then blend again with the electric mixer.

❻ Turn into the prepared soufflé dishes and chill until set.

❼ To serve, carefully remove collar around the dishes and top with pomegranate seeds or with lemon and lime strips.

● Makes 4 to 6 servings.

Heavenly Lychee Soufflé

A light, exotic and heavenly dessert!

Iced Honeydew Yogurt

Preparation time: 10 min.
Freezing time: 20 min.+

½ large honeydew melon, peeled and seeded
2 cups (500 mL) plain yogurt
½ cup + 2 tbsp. (130 g) sugar
1 tsp. lemon juice
1 tsp. lime juice
½ tsp. powdered ginger
1¼ tsp. almond extract
2 tbsp. lemonade, from concentrate
Mint leaves (to garnish)

❶ Chop half of the melon coarsely. Scoop out balls from the remaining honeydew using a Parisian cutter and set aside.

❷ Place the chopped honeydew together with remaining ingredients, except the mint leaves, in an electric blender and process at high speed until smoothly puréed.

❸ Pour into an ice-cream maker and freeze according to the manufacturer's instructions (20 minutes). If you do not own one, refer to the recipe "Orange Ice Cream", page 109 for regular freezing procedures.

❹ To serve, garnish with the reserved honeydew balls (frosted, if desired), and some mint leaves.

● Makes 4½ cups (1 litre).

Cocktails and Punches

Exotic Fizz and Grape Fizz (page 133)

Royal Papaya

Preparation time: 5 min.

1/3 cup diced papaya
1 1/2 oz. (45 mL) grapefruit juice
1 1/2 oz. (45 mL) pineapple juice
1 tbsp. light cream
1 tbsp. grenadine
1 1/2 oz. (45 mL) cherry liqueur (optional)
2 oz. (60 mL) Club Soda
1/3 cup crushed ice
Pinch of cinnamon
1 small papaya slice (to garnish)

❶ Place the first six ingredients in an electric blender and mix at high speed for a few seconds until smooth.

❷ Pour into a tall glass; add Club Soda. Fill with crushed ice and stir.

❸ Sprinkle with cinnamon and garnish with the papaya slice.

❹ Serve with a straw.

● Makes 1 serving.

Pears Abroad (page 131)   Island Caress (page 131)   Royal Papaya (above)

Island Caress

Preparation time: 5 min.

3 oz. (90 mL) grapefruit juice
4 oz. (120 mL) pineapple juice
2 oz. (60 mL) guava juice
1 oz. (30 mL) dark rum (optional)
2 tsp. extra-fine sugar
1 tbsp. light cream
1/3 cup crushed ice
1 tsp. ground nuts
1 carambola slice (to garnish)

❶ Put all the ingredients except the crushed ice, the nuts and the carambola slice in an electric blender and mix at high speed for a few seconds.

❷ Pour into a tall glass, then add the crushed ice. Top with ground nuts and garnish with the carambola slice.

❸ Serve with a straw.

● Makes 1 serving.

Pears Abroad

Preparation time: 8 min.

1 ripe pear, peeled
2 oz. (60 mL) pineapple juice
1 oz. (30 mL) apple juice concentrate
1 oz. (30 mL) white grape juice
1/3 cup crushed ice
1 tbsp. calvados (optional)
1 oz. (30 mL) Club Soda

❶ Core the pear and put aside 2 thin slices to garnish. Cut the rest into small pieces.

❷ Put the pieces of pear and the fruit juices in an electric blender and whirl on high speed until mixture is smooth and creamy.

❸ Pour into a tall glass over crushed ice, then add calvados and Club Soda.

❹ Garnish with the reserved pear slices and serve with double straws.

● Makes 1 serving.

Summer Cup

Preparation time: 10 min.

2 peaches, cut into small pieces
1 nectarine, cut into small pieces
12 halved strawberries
4 cups (1 litre) light sparkling cider
¼ cup (60 mL) sherry
⅓ cup (60 g) extra-fine sugar
1 tbsp. lemon juice
Plenty of ice cubes

❶ Toss the fruit into a salad bowl or punch bowl.

❷ Pour the cider and sherry over the fruit.

❸ Add sugar and lemon juice; stir until sugar is dissolved.

❹ Add plenty of ice cubes and let stand 30 minutes before serving.

● Makes 6 to 8 servings.

Exotic Fizz

Preparation time: 5 min.

1/3 cup crushed ice
1/2 cup (125 mL) exotic fruit-juice mix
1 tbsp. coconut cream syrup
1 tbsp. light cream
1 1/2 oz. (45 mL) cherry liqueur (optional)
Club Soda to fill the glass
1 maraschino cherry (to garnish)
1 piece of pineapple (to garnish)

❶ Place the ice in a tall glass.

❷ Put the fruit-juice mix, coconut cream syrup, light cream and cherry liqueur in an electric blender and mix at high speed for a few seconds.

❸ Pour into the glass and fill with Club Soda.

❹ Garnish with the maraschino cherry and the piece of pineapple.

❺ Serve with a straw.

• Makes 1 serving.

See photograph on page 129.

Grape Fizz

Preparation time: 5 min.

3 oz. (90 mL) grape nectar, chilled
1 tsp. extra-fine sugar
1 egg white
1 1/2 oz. (45 mL) dark rum (optional)
1/3 cup crushed ice
2 oz. (60 mL) ginger ale, chilled
A few red grapes (to garnish)

❶ Put all the ingredients except crushed ice, ginger ale, and red grapes in an electric blender. Mix at high speed for a few seconds.

❷ Pour into a tall glass over crushed ice. Slowly add the ginger ale.

❸ Garnish with 1 or 2 red grapes on a cocktail skewer and serve with a straw.

• Makes 1 serving.

See photograph on page 129.

Papaya Punch

Preparation time: 10 min.

1 ripe papaya, peeled, seeded and diced (reserve some to garnish)
2 cups (500 mL) pineapple juice, chilled
1 cup (250 mL) grapefruit juice, chilled
1 1/2 cups (375 mL) apple juice, chilled
3/4 cup (140 g) extra-fine sugar
1 cup (250 mL) white rum (optional)
Nutmeg
1 cup (250 mL) ginger ale, chilled

❶ A day before, prepare an ice block by freezing water (that has been boiled and cooled**) in a round medium-sized decorative mold.

❷ Put the diced papaya and pineapple juice in an electric blender and mix for a few seconds until smooth. Pour into a salad bowl or a punch bowl and add the remaining ingredients with the exception of nutmeg and ginger ale. Mix slowly.

❸ Unmold the ice block and carefully place in the bowl.

❹ Let stand 5 minutes, then add the reserved diced papaya. Sprinkle with nutmeg.

❺ When ready to serve, gently pour the ginger ale down the side of the bowl and mix slowly.

● Makes about 16 - 4 oz. (125 mL) servings.

** Boiling removes dissolved air. Freezing previously boiled water gives a block of ice that is clearer and more transparent.

REMARK: *This punch is equally delicious without rum. Children will be able to taste and enjoy the punch as much as adults. Rum can be added on an individual basis.*

Orangina Punch

Preparation time: 7 min.

1 - 750 mL bottle Orangina, chilled
1 - 12 oz. (341 mL) can frozen lemonade concentrate, thawed
2 cups (500 mL) pineapple juice, chilled
2 cups (500 mL) Cointreau (optional)
½ cup (100 g) extra-fine sugar
2 cups (500 mL) Club Soda, chilled
5 scoops orange ice cream (see recipe, page 109)
Pinch of cinnamon
Pinch of nutmeg

❶ A day before, prepare an ice ring by freezing water (that has been boiled and cooled**) in a Savarin mold or in any other ring mold.

❷ In a punch bowl or a large salad bowl, combine Orangina, lemonade, pineapple juice and Cointreau.

❸ Add sugar and stir slowly till dissolved. Chill.

❹ When ready to serve, pour the Club Soda slowly down the side of the bowl and stir gently.

❺ Unmold the ice ring and carefully place in the bowl. Top with scoops of orange ice cream and sprinkle with cinnamon and nutmeg.

❻ Stir gently and let the ice cream melt slightly before serving.

• Makes 22 to 24 - 4 oz. (125 mL) servings.

** Boiling removes dissolved air. Freezing previously boiled water gives a block of ice that is clearer and more transparent.

Celebration Grape Punch

Preparation time: 10 min.

4 cups (1 litre) unsweetened grape juice, chilled
1 - 12 oz. (341 mL) can frozen lemonade concentrate, thawed
¼ cup (60 mL) grenadine
Plenty of ice cubes
Slices of fresh fruits in season
1 - 750 mL bottle of champagne, chilled
3 scoops of vanilla ice cream (see recipe, page 99)
Pinch of cinnamon
Pinch of nutmeg

❶ In a punch bowl or salad bowl, combine the grape juice with lemonade. Pour in the grenadine; blend well.

❷ Add plenty of ice cubes and slices of fresh fruits.

❸ Slowly pour the champagne down the side of the bowl. Top with scoops of vanilla ice cream.

❹ Sprinkle cinnamon and nutmeg atop. Let the ice cream melt slightly and stir gently before serving.

● Makes 22 to 24 - 4 oz. (125 mL) servings.

REMARK: *This colorful, easy-to-prepare punch has a very special blend of flavors which will thrill your guests.*

Sweet Island Punch

Preparation time: 12 min.

- 4 cups (1 litre) apple juice (to make the ice ring)
- 1 - 8 oz. (225 mL) can pineapple ring slices, drained
- 2 cups (500 mL) pineapple juice, chilled
- 1 cup (250 mL) grapefruit juice, chilled
- 1 - 12½ oz. (355 mL) can frozen apple juice concentrate, thawed
- 2 cups (500 mL) cream soda, chilled
- 2 cups (500 mL) bitter lemon, chilled
- 1 - 14 oz. (398 mL) can pineapple chunks
- 2 cups (500 mL) dark rum (optional)
- 3 scoops pineapple sherbet (see recipe, page 124)
- 1 tbsp. ground nuts

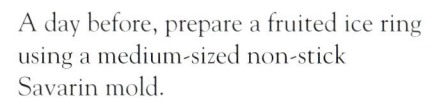

A day before, prepare a fruited ice ring using a medium-sized non-stick Savarin mold.

❶ To prepare the fruited ice ring, pour apple juice in the mold to a depth of ½ inch (12 mm). Freeze, then arrange the pineapple rings in the mold in a decorative pattern and press lightly to make the pineapple rings take the shape of the mold. Add apple juice to partially cover the pineapples and put back in the freezer. When solidified, fill the mold with apple juice and let freeze overnight.

❷ Combine all the remaining fruit juices in a punch bowl. Slowly add cream soda and bitter lemon.

❸ Open the can of pineapple chunks and pour the entire contents into the punch bowl.

❹ Add the rum and mix well.

❺ Unmold the ring and slowly place it in the punch bowl.

❻ Top with scoops of sherbet (inside the fruited ice ring) and sprinkle with ground nuts.

❼ Let stand 5 minutes. Stir gently before serving.

● Makes 24 - 4 oz. (125 mL) servings.

Summer Peach Flavored Jelly Punch

Preparation time: 12 min.

2 - 3 oz. (85 g) jelly powder packages, peach flavor
(4 cups) 1 litre apple juice, chilled
(4 cups) 1 litre pineapple juice, chilled
1 - 12 oz. (341 mL) can frozen orange juice concentrate, thawed
½ cup (105 g) extra-fine sugar
1 cup (250 mL) calvados (optional)
2 cups (500 mL) ginger ale, chilled

❶ A day before, prepare a large block of ice by freezing water (that has been boiled and cooled**) in a round decorative 5 or 6-inch (13 or 15-cm) mold.

❷ Then, prepare the jelly according to directions given on the package, using a mold of your choice and allow to firm overnight. When set, unmold carefully, then cut into ½-inch (1.25-cm) cubes.

❸ Combine all the fruit juices in a punch bowl, then add sugar. Stir until dissolved.

❹ Unmold the block of ice and place carefully in the punch bowl. Add calvados, jelly cubes, and slowly pour in ginger ale. Stir.

❺ Let stand 5 minutes before serving.

● Makes 27 to 29 - 4 oz. (125 mL) servings.

** Boiling removes dissolved air. Freezing previously boiled water gives a block of ice that is clearer and more transparent.

REMARK: *The peach flavored jelly cubes are a pleasant surprise. Also, ideal for children's parties; simply omit the calvados.*

Tropical Punch

Preparation time: 12 min.

1 large watermelon
1 cup (250 mL) grapefruit juice, chilled
3 cups (750 mL) pineapple juice, chilled
1 - 12½ oz. (355 mL) can frozen apple juice concentrate, thawed
2 cups (500 mL) Club Soda, chilled
2 cups (500 mL) dark rum (optional)
Plenty of ice cubes

❶ Cut the melon in half. Remove seeds from the pulp of one half of the watermelon. Chop enough pulp in order to obtain two and a half cups of purée.

❷ Scoop out balls with the remaining half of the watermelon using a Parisian cutter and set aside (remove seeds).

❸ Put plenty of ice cubes in a punch bowl or a salad bowl and pour in the fruit juices along with the puréed watermelon. Add the watermelon balls. Stir.

❹ Slowly pour in the Club Soda and the rum. Stir gently.

● Makes 24 - 4 oz. (125 mL) servings.

ALTERNATIVE: *Serving this punch in a watermelon shell will add a tropical touch to your party. To do so, choose a melon that is of spherical shape. Slice ⅓ off the upper part of the watermelon and then scoop out balls from half the pulp of the bottom part. Carefully hollow it out and afterwards, trim the base to make it steady. Cut the edge of the melon into vandykes (serrated).*

Night Dream

Preparation time: 7 min.

¼ cup diced mango pulp
1 oz. (30 mL) grapefruit juice
2 oz. (60 mL) papaya juice (or papaya drink or papaya nectar)
1 oz. (30 mL) pineapple juice
1 oz. (30 mL) orange juice
1 tbsp. grenadine
1½ oz. (45 mL) dark rum (optional)
⅓ cup crushed ice
1 mango slice (to garnish)

❶ Place all the ingredients with the exception of the crushed ice, and the mango slice in an electric blender and mix at high speed for a few seconds until smooth and creamy.

❷ Pour into a tall glass over crushed ice.

❸ Garnish with the mango slice and serve with a straw.

● Makes 1 serving.

REMARK: If you wish to prepare several servings at the same time, simply multiply the measures by the number of guests present.

Burst of Passion (page 141) *Night Dream (above)* *Mysterious Avocado Cream (page 141)*

Mysterious Avocado Cream

Preparation time: 5 min.

1/2 cup crushed ice
1/4 cup diced avocado
2 oz. (60 mL) pineapple juice
1 oz. (30 mL) grapefruit juice
1 oz. (30 mL) apple juice concentrate
1/2 oz. (15 mL) lemonade concentrate
1 tbsp. light cream
1 tsp. coconut cream syrup
1 oz. (30 mL) dark rum (optional)
1 tsp. sweetened shredded coconut
1 avocado slice (to garnish)

❶ Put the crushed ice in a tall glass.

❷ Place the remaining ingredients except the shredded coconut and the avocado slice in an electric blender and process at high speed for a few seconds until smooth and creamy.

❸ Pour into the glass over the crushed ice and sprinkle with shredded coconut.

❹ Garnish with the avocado slice on a cocktail skewer and serve with a straw.

• Makes 1 serving.

Burst of Passion

Preparation time: 4 min.

1/3 cup crushed ice
1/2 banana, crushed
2 oz. (60 mL) orange juice
2 oz. (60 mL) pineapple juice
1 oz. (30 mL) grapefruit juice
1 tbsp. light cream
1 tbsp. grenadine
1 tsp. ground nuts
1 1/2 oz. (45 mL) dark rum (optional)
A few banana slices (to garnish)

❶ Place the crushed ice in a tall glass.

❷ Put the remaining ingredients except the banana slices in an electric blender and mix at high speed for a few seconds until smooth and creamy.

❸ Pour into the glass and garnish with two or three banana slices on a cocktail skewer or a straw.

• Makes 1 serving.

REMARK: This makes a welcome, festive drink for children. Rich in flavor, it is definitely a children's favorite. Just omit the rum. Adults will also appreciate its tanginess.

INDEX

Page

Canapés - Hors d'Oeuvres - Sandwiches

Avocado Canapés	11
Beef Tartlets	28
Brococrab Mousse	14
Cheesy Zucchini Balls	9
Chicken-Celery Sandwich	24
Chicken-Bacon Sandwich	23
Crab and Fish Pâté	21
Cucumber-Ham Appetizers	16
Flic-en-Flac Pouches	17
Mont Choisy Rolled-up Bites	8
Oriental Beef and Pepper Sandwich	22
Salmon and Egg Sandwich	25
Sausages with Honeydew and Cantaloup	27
Smoked Oyster Canapés	13
Tarragon Meat Pouches	19
Tropical Meatballs	10
Tuna and Tomato Sandwich	26
Yellow Pea Rings — "Gâteau Pima"	6

Salads

Artichoke-Corn Salad	34
Avocado Salad with Peanut Butter Vinaigrette	30
Beet and Potato Egg Salad	35
Carambola Star Salad	32
Hearts-of-Palm Island Salad	36
Okra Salad	31
Tropical Salad	31
Water Chestnut Salad	33

Soups

Cauliflower Soup with Crab	40
Chayote Soup with Clams	39
Chinese Bean Curd Soup	42
Crab Soup with Vegetables	41
Cream of Corn and Leek Soup	38
Spinach Soup with Fish	39

Main Dishes

	Page
Asparagus-Chicken Soufflé	94
Butterfly Pork Chops with Leek	61
Chayote-Beef Casserole	47
Chayote Flan	65
Chicken Curry with Eggplant and Kidney Beans	46
Chicken in Mango Sauce	77
Chicken with Creamy Spinach	81
Chicken with Two Types of Mushrooms	80
Chinese Fried Rice	69
Chinese Sautéed Vegetables	51
Chinese Spare-Ribs	50
Chinese Steamed Fresh Fish	74
Curried Fish Steaks	57
Fisherman's Cauliflower	49
Island Papaya Fried Rice	45
Marylin's Pineapple Chicken	72
Marylin's Vermicelli	90
Morne Brabant Crêpes with Chicken and Chayote	54
Oriental Fish with Noodles and Vegetables	75
Oriental Style Sliced Beef	51
Pirate's Beef Liver with Pepper	66
Poached Salmon with Chestnut Sauce	58
Pork Roast with Honey and Cloves	92
Salted Cod Flan	71
Seafood Crêpes	53
Seafood with Papaya	67
Sole Fillets with Shrimp-Tomato Sauce	62
Sun Fried Rice	78
Sweet and Sour Beef Liver with Radishes	63
Tomato Rice	69
Touessrok Sliced Pork Legs	56
Trou-aux-Biches Fisherman's Plate	44
Veal Roast with Pears	86
Veal Rolls with Black Beans - Chinese Style	88
Veal Scallops with Prunes	59
Veal Shanks with Grapes	84
Zucchini-Shrimp Quiche	83

Desserts

Banana Beignets des Alizés	96
Banana-Coconut Ring Cake	97
Cheese-Chestnut Tart	102
Corn Pudding with Coconut	111
Creamy Pineapple Cheesecake	106
Grenadine Watermelon Mousse	110
Guava Ice Cream	101
Guava Soufflé	125
Heavenly Lychee Soufflé	127
Iced Honeydew Yogurt	128
Island Fruit Salad	117
Orange-Chocolate Mousse Cake	119
Mango Parfait	115
Orange Ice Cream	109
Orange Sauce	121
Peach Shortcake	122
Pineapple Sherbet	124
Pear Flan	116
Riche-Terre Pineapple Crêpes	104
Shortcake with Chestnut Cream	113
Stuffed Lychees with Orange Cream and Watermelon Sauce	99
Tropical-Sun Cake	107
Vanilla Ice Cream	99

Cocktails and Punches

Burst of Passion	141
Celebration Grape Punch	136
Exotic Fizz	133
Grape Fizz	133
Island Caress	131
Mysterious Avocado Cream	141
Night Dream	140
Orangina Punch	135
Papaya Punch	134
Pears Abroad	131
Royal Papaya	130
Summer Cup	132
Summer Peach Flavored Jelly Punch	138
Sweet Island Punch	137
Tropical Punch	139